Winning Head Races

Carlo Zezza

--- Saving Seconds on a Long Row ---

Winning Head Races

Copyright © 2015 by Carlo Zezza

ISBN 978-0-578-16274-4

Additional copies of this book may be purchased at www.winningheadraces.com

All rights reserved.

No part of this book may be reproduced without written permission from the copyright holder, except for a reviewer who may quote brief passages in a review; nor may any part of this book be reproduced, stored in a retrieval system, or transmitted in any form or by any means electronic mechanical, photocopying, recording, or other, without written permission from the copyright holder.

Acknowledgments

Most of this book is based on shared experience. We can all be grateful, as I am, for the open spirit that characterizes our sport.

Several individuals generously devoted time and attention through iterations of the draft manuscript. I am especially grateful to Ted Van Dusen for sharing his test data and his knowledge on boats, fins, and boat weight, to Gregg Stone, whose unique insights are reflected in several sections, to Rick Anderson and Greg Benning, for their wisdom on rowing a winding course, and to Henry Hamilton and Gordon Hamilton, who were both kind enough to read through the draft with me in person.

For their meticulous word-by-word review, I thank John Flory and Henry Francis, who individually acted as volunteer editors. Henry's viewpoint was sharpened by his first Head Of The Charles participation, shortly before seeing an early draft of this book (he finished creditably above his bow number).

For their big-boat perspective, I thank Andy Anderson, aka Doctor Rowing, as well as Charley Butt and Patrick Lapage at Harvard, who made an invaluable contribution – a winding river is not the same at the speed of an elite eight.

I am grateful to Fred Schoch, Executive Director of the Head Of The Charles®, for his comments on this greatest of regattas, and to Michael Joyner, MD, of the Mayo Clinic, for his review and green light on the sections concerning Training for Long Distance and Strength Training.

Thanks are also due, and not only for this book, to Margarita, my wife and training partner, for her knowledge about conditioning, and for setting an example of efficient technique.

For any errors of fact or mistaken opinion, the individuals noted above are blameless. If such exist, they are my own.

Contents

	page
Preface / Small Boats and Big Boats	1
Racing the Clock	2
Pacing	3
Boats and Fins	11
Oars and Rigging	21
Weight	25
Navigation	
-- Learning the Course	27
-- Mirror	28
-- Turning	30
-- Risk-Reward	38
Traffic	
-- Seeding & the Accordion	42
-- Passing	43
-- Taking the Inside	44
-- Being passed	47
-- S-bends	49
-- Avoiding Contact	53
-- Collisions	58
Training for Long Distance	65
Race Preparation	75
Summing Up	77

Appendix:

I. Strength Training	79
II. Starting with the Mirror	83
III. Stake Turn Technique	87
IV. More About Fins	93
V. Course Notes	99

-- Armada Cup	Wohlensee, Bern
-- Silverskiff	Po River, Turin
-- Scullers' Head of the River	Tideway, London
-- Head Of The Charles	Charles River, Boston

Preface

More individuals in the USA participate in head races than in side-by-side course races, but matters specific to head racing don't get much attention.

Boat builders pursue optimal performance in side-by-side racing. Most training is aimed at speed over relatively short courses, one or two kilometers.

In a head race, rowing fast can offset many mistakes, but sharing a long, winding course raises issues which don't exist for racing side by side in a straight line. The best finish time is often decided by pacing for long distance, rowing the best course, and managing obstacles, notably including other boats.

There is no substitute for good coaching, and an abundance of literature concerns rowing technique and training for speed.

"Winning Head Races" is intended to fill in "all the rest".

Small Boats and Big Boats

While "Winning Head Races" is written by a sculler, most observations and suggestions apply equally to eights and fours.

Published wisdom for coxed crews burdens the cox with turns and traffic, while rowers just row. Chapters on Navigation and Traffic suggest that these areas, like everything else in rowing, call for teamwork from the entire crew.

> Comments specific to big boats are outlined in blue

Racing the Clock

Racing against the clock is mentally harder than racing side-by-side, because pressure must come from within, over the full length of a long course, not knowing your position in the race.

Rowers new to head racing may feel uncomfortable with the mental demands of a long row to beat the clock. Younger rowers, especially those coming from side-by-side school sprints, may miss the quick gratification of closure at the finish line.

Preference for one or the other is a matter of taste. For many rowers, the complex challenges of a head race more than compensate for the simpler pleasure of racing side-by-side.

Pacing

The best pace is the maximum average that is sustainable for the entire course.

For pacing a long race, it's helpful to understand the exponential relation of power to speed:

Power³ = Speed

In practical terms, increasing boat speed 5% (e.g. from 4 meters/second to 4.2 meters/second) requires a power increase of 16%.

Rowing faster than the max sustainable pace costs extra energy for little reward. It's not worth it, except for sprinting at the end of the race, and for short bursts supported by ATP-CP (for ATP-CP, please read on).

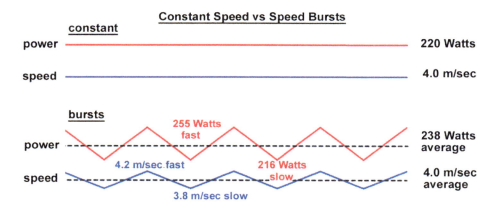

The two plots, one constant and the other with speed bursts, have the same average speed. But the plot with speed bursts costs more in effort, +18 Watts.[1]

Muscles get their power from complex processes, that overlap and intermingle in the course of a race. The following is a simplification that is useful for training and for racing. Power comes from:

1) **Oxygen** from the bloodstream. Oxygen is the main and only sustainable source for endurance racing ("aerobic exercise").

When the supply of oxygen can't support the effort, ...

2) **Glycolysis** from blood glucose (essentially, sugar) or muscle glycogen (the stored form of glucose) makes up the difference.

  A byproduct of using glucose is lactic acid – the "burn". Burning muscles lead quickly to burn out. For most of us, expect burn out at full pressure in less than 1 minute.

Max sustainable pace is somewhere at the top limit of the aerobic system, i.e. at the top of your Anaerobic Threshold ("**AT**"). [2]

... AT can be pegged to heart rate (HR) with lactate testing[3] but 'cardiac creep' sends HR higher than test values: After 20+ minutes of racing, HR may be 20 beats higher than an AT peg determined by 7 or 8 minutes on an erg. <u>Pace</u> is a better measure of energy cost than HR, unless you are familiar with your HR behavior during races.

To find max sustainable pace, Gordon Hamilton[4] suggests testing at full pressure on 2 kilometer pieces. If you can go for 2k, you can probably continue for 5k or more. Consider Gordon's remarks on the psychology of effort – once into the race, don't worry about getting to the end, you won't feel any worse at the end than you feel at the moment.

The subject of pacing is, in fact, a knotty issue. Many beginning racers are concerned about getting to the end, and don't work as hard as they could for fear of collapse before the finish. Gordon's advice is especially appropriate for them.

By contrast with Gordon's advice, experienced head racers tend to counsel caution, especially in the first minutes of a long race.

Pace is best measured by perceived effort, with HR input from the heart rate monitor. Wind can make an enormous difference in pace measured by a speed monitor[5], and current can also make a difference for a GPS system. Perception of effort and HR expectations are gained by rowing long pieces, full-length time trials, and warmup races, to feel how much pressure your body can sustain.

3) The third power source is **ATP-CP**, combining 'adenosine triphosphate' and 'creatine phosphate' . Another name for the same thing is the Phosphagen System.

ATP-CP is instantaneous, potent, and good for only 9 to 10 seconds of high intensity effort, i.e. 5 or 6 strokes at full pressure. ATP-CP puts no load on the aerobic system, and using ATP-CP has no lasting energy cost.

In short races (1 to 2 kilometers, 4 to 8 minutes), intense effort at the start inevitably exhausts ATP-CP, draws energy from glucose, and creates a lactic acid burden which the rower must support throughout the race, right into the sprint at the end – sprint racers don't have the option of waiting for their cardiovascular system to get up to speed.

Carrying a similar lactic acid accumulation for 20+ minutes is a daunting prospect, and will reduce your ability to pull before you reach the finish line. Even if your resistance to pain is unlimited, the energy cost of a speedy start will be deducted from your output through the race.

Use ATP-CP to get up to race speed **before you cross the start line,** and **no faster**.[6] Your cardio-vascular system will take time to ramp up, and once your ATP-CP is exhausted, your muscles must call on glucose, with rapidly ensuing burn. In a long race, don't sprint at the start. Give your cardio-vascular system time to catch up.[7]

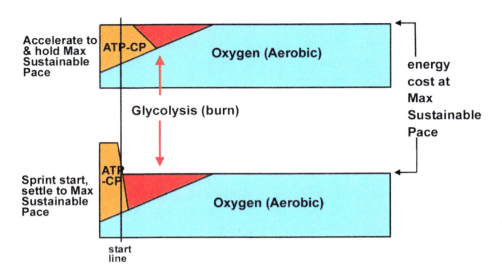

In the diagram above, the orange areas labeled 'ATP-CP' are identical in size, representing the finite limit of ATP-CP before exhaustion. The sprint start's 'Glycolysis' red area is 60% greater than the 'Glycolysis' area in the accelerate & hold start, representing 60% added burden on the anaerobic system, i.e. "burn".

ATP-CP recovers with time, depending on energy output. At rest, ATP-CP recovers in about 2 minutes (effort:recovery time = ± 1 : 10).

With continued intense effort, ATP-CP won't replenish at all.

After 7 or 8 minutes, with effort at the high end of AT (as in a head race of 20+ minutes), some ATP-CP is restored to support brief bursts of effort. (No studies are found concerning recovery time for ATP-CP while exercising at anaerobic threshold; these comments are based on racing experience.)

Many crews employ "power tens". These brief intense efforts can draw on ATP-CP for energy. Read the following section on turns and traffic, and see if there aren't intelligent ways to call on your ATP-CP.

Sprinting

At the end of any race the energy bucket should be empty.

Most opinions agree to start sprinting (stroke rate up and effort at max) with about 300 meters to go, i.e. 45 to 50 strokes from the finish.[8] By the finish line, or maybe a little before, ATP-CP resources will be long gone, you will be running on glucose, and the burn will start shutting down your muscles' ability to move the boat.

For most of us, to start sprinting more than 300 or 400 meters from the end risks an involuntary slowdown before the finish. Start sprinting late, and you will finish some seconds slower than your potential.

Notes to Pacing

Note 1 – The graph is intended to show the relation of effort to speed, not precise values. Watts vs meters/second is a rough estimation, based on perceived effort in a single scull compared with the erg. On the erg, Watts vs meters/second relate to rowing in an eight, but the relationship of effort to speed remains the same.

Note 2 - Training to elevate anaerobic threshold is vital, well-documented, and outside the range of this book. A good coach can advise.

Note 3 – the maximum heart rate formula, "225 less your age", was invented by a couple of doctors based on unsupported speculation, and somehow absorbed into the culture of sports training. Heart rate does descend with age, but individuals vary greatly. For trained elder athletes, maximum heart rate can exceed the formula maximum by 20% or more; for some, in later decades, heart rate hardly descends at all.

To know maximum heart rate, Gordon Hamilton suggests rowing a series of intervals at increasing pressure, on the erg or in the boat. Start with a 10-minute warmup. Then row 30" on and 30" off until your heart rate stops increasing. This is a tough workout and needs to fit in your training plan. Another way is to look at your heart rate monitor just after finishing a long head race – your heart rate should be at maximum if you have sprinted to the finish.

Knowing maximum heart rate is only important for calculating target heart rates at different training levels – for anaerobic threshold and for aerobic workouts. These levels can be better determined with lactate testing.

Note 4 – Gordon Hamilton, *Sculling in a Nutshell*, Amazon, 2013

Note 5 – Don't make the mistake of averaging pace for tail and head winds. Headwinds hurt far more than tailwinds help. Apparent wind is reduced or increased by boat speed. Wind force varies as **the cube of wind velocity**. A 4 mph headwind gives an adverse apparent wind of ± 13 mph while a 4 mph tailwind gives an adverse apparent wind of ± 5 mph. The difference in adverse force is 18x! (because of the cubic exponential relation).

Note 6 – Some winning racers counsel starting a little slower than race pace. In the Dec '14 issue of Rowing News, for 6k erg tests, Volker Nolte writes that "many recommend negative splitting. Start out one to two seconds slower per 500 meters than where you want to end up at the end of the piece, and lower your splits by one second every 1,000 meters, ...

Note 7 - Pre-race warmup should prime your cardio-vascular system to respond. Different physiologies work in different ways, and it's worth experimenting on pre-race routines. Try 20 or 30 strokes at race pace, until your HR rises into your AT zone,. This will accelerate cardio-vascular response after the race starts.

Once warmed up, my cardio-vascular system can remember the call over a surprisingly long rest time, 10 or 15 minutes, observed from gym experiments as well as experience on the water.

Note 8 – Dr Fritz Hagerman, long-time physiological advisor to USRowing, says "the Lactic Acid System's range of maximum energy production is 60-90 seconds during high intensity exercise." The shorter 60 second end of the range corresponds to personal experience. Dr Fritz Hagerman – "Training the Energy Systems" – on the internet.

Boats and Fins

Don't change your boat

The best boat for head racing is the one you are most comfortable rowing, in the most likely race conditions.

Naval architects trade between low wetted surface, stability, and sea-keeping qualities. Recent-era shells have tended to be less like needles and more like spheres[1], so that they have less wetted surface. Less wetted surface means less skin drag, and boats with low wetted surface feel slippery as they run between strokes. They also can seem nervous and twitchy, to rowers who are accustomed to boats with more skin in the water.

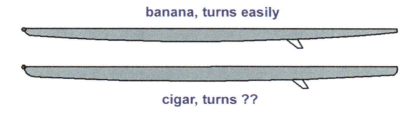

Some hulls are more banana-shaped, i.e. their bottoms curve up at the bow and stern (in surfer parlance, they have more scoop and rocker). Other hulls are more cigar-shaped, relatively flat from bow to stern, fuller and deeper at the ends. Banana-shaped boats turn easier in a shorter radius. Cigar-shaped boats tend to feel more stable.

Rowers are 3 to 7 times heavier than their boats. A boat loaded more heavily than intended will have increased wetted surface and a lowered center of gravity. The overloaded boat will feel more stable than a boat loaded to its design weight.

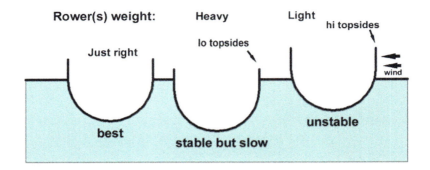

... It seems counter-intuitive, but an overloaded lightweight boat can feel steadier than a heavyweight boat carrying rowers of design weight. Increased stability from overloading the boat does not provide more speed. [2]

A good question is whether a lightly loaded big boat isn't potentially fast – the answer is probably 'yes', but only if the boat's balance and direction can be controlled without losing efficiency. Where wind and wave conditions are difficult, a boat that is too big (or rowers too light for the boat) will be moved around by waves and wind, and require more technique to control. Flat water favors lightly loaded boats with low wetted surface, that have less skin drag.

Behavior in rough water is strongly influenced by the contours of the hull as well as its wetted surface. As a matter of opinion, speed in rough water and high wind is more influenced by good sea-keeping. Speed in flat conditions is more influenced by low wetted surface. If most of your head racing is likely to be in windy, difficult conditions, e.g. the Tideway in London, favor sea-keeping. Winding courses like the Head Of The Charles®, where waves don't build up and the banks provide some shelter from the wind, favor slippery boats with low wetted surface.

> While the preceding comments are directed to singles and doubles, hydrodynamics are no different for eights and fours. The main difference is that crews of large boats may not have a choice of craft and it may not be possible to match crew weight to the ideal load of their boat.

The effect of boat weight *per se* is a matter of discussion, and some nonsense. Please see the section on "Weight".

What about the fin?

Ask what the fin is for, and the most likely answer will be that it makes the boat go straight. **In a race with turns, is that what you want?** The perfect fin should:

Reduce turning effort to a minimum

Set direction straight when the oars are out of the water

Resist wind drift without weather cocking

Slide through sunken debris

Appendix IV – "More on Fins" offers background on these qualities.

Boat builders have **no** incentive to make a head racing fin.[3] Their main concern is that boats should not weather cock in crosswinds, which can result in an overlarge fin. Skin drag is considerable (a fin has two sides) but is often ignored.

The next photo shows a 'head race special' fin that is easy to turn, and that snaps a single straight on recovery. The surface area is 76 cm^2, smaller than all stock fins except the fins on Carl Douglas boats.

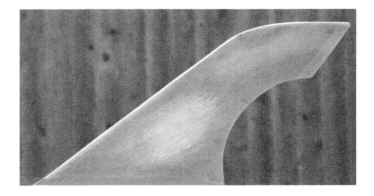

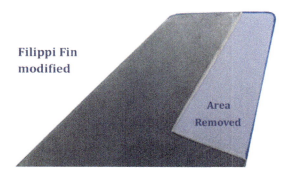

Aluminum is easy to cut. A simple zigzag cut with a hacksaw can remove about a third of the surface of a standard fin. The photo above shows a cut Filippi fin, compared to the Filippi stock fin. The cut Van Dusen and Filippi fins were used in the comparison with stock fins described next.

An easy-turning fin is worth seconds in a head race with turns. The following values are approximate, but the relationship is clear.[4] The table predicts the time for a good Masters single sculler on the Head Of The Charles course, with a selection of fins.

Total time:		
	banana hull	cigar hull
Stock fin	20:22	20:33
Cut fin	20:17	20:24
Difference from stock	5 sec's	9 sec's
'cigar' stock vs 'banana' cut --> 16 sec's		
(64 meters @ 4 m/sec!)		

The cut fin tested on the cigar-shaped hull is smaller than the stock fin on the banana-shaped hull, but the cigar-shaped hull is harder to turn. The stock fin on the cigar-shaped hull is huge and, combined with the hull, very hard to turn.

Except in a strong crosswind, where drift and weather cocking are the main concern, a smaller-than-stock fin has only positive effects for head racing.[5]

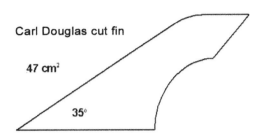

This scalloped fin is about 20% smaller than the already small Carl Douglas stock fin. This fin tracks straight and does not weather cock.

Hull, fin, and rower weight are all involved in choosing or making a head racing fin. A fin that is perfect on one hull may not be ideal on another. Lighter rowers may need a bigger fin.

... A cigar shaped hull (harder to turn) can use a smaller fin. A banana shaped hull may need a larger fin. Larger fins may be needed for crosswinds.

... The weight of the rower(s) influences the ideal size of the fin. A Van Dusen mid-weight double was rowed at the Head Of The Charles by two women whose weight did not sink the boat to the ends. They could not row straight with the Van Dusen single fin (the fins are interchangeable), and raced with the standard double fin. They were very fast in the lightly loaded boat – credit their technique – and set a course record.

On most head race courses with a normally weighted hull, a smaller fin works as well on a double as on a single. Heavier crews raced the Van

Dusen double in the preceding paragraph with the single fin, and also won.

Doubles present more topside to the wind, and are more subject to drift and weathercocking. But crosswinds are rare on head race courses, where wind is channeled up and down stream by the river banks.[6]

> **Big boats with rudders can also benefit from a smaller fin**. For head racing, eights should be fitted with a smaller fin, typically with a fin for a coxed four. For winding courses in Holland, Dutch eights are fitted with **a big rudder and a small fin.**
>
> Although this change is simply done, only a few USA coaches alter their eights and fours for head races. This is an easy opportunity for improved finish times.
>
> For quads and fours, Carl Douglas offers a unique and ingenious solution to steering and crosswind drift. The fin is also a rudder, because of its flexible, controllable trailing edge. A second fin is mounted forward, under the 2-seat. The boat pivots around the forward fin for easy turns, the integrated rudder-fin minimizes drag, and the combination strongly resists sideways pressure from crosswinds. Added skin drag from the forward fin offsets some of the advantage of this arrangement.

A last word on fins: For races with a **stake turn** (any sharp turn around a buoy or buoys), [7] an oversize stock fin is painful and very slow. Please see Appendix III – "Stake Turn Technique."

Changing your boat, just for head racing, isn't common sense for most of us. Changing the fin is easy. Most people with access to a shop can do it themselves, and many boat builders will comply with special requests.[8]

For head racing... **CHANGE YOUR FIN**

Notes to Boats and Fins

Note 1 – A sphere contains the most volume for its surface. A needle contains almost no volume for its surface. In the text "banana" is used for boats which are more akin to spheres, "cigar" is used for boats that are more akin to needles. For the rower, the difference is a matter of feeling – sphere-ish is more lively, like driving a Mini, needle-ish is more steady, like driving a bus.

Note 2 – In 1998 Resolute launched new lightweight and heavyweight singles. The crossover rower weight was 80kg (i.e. at 80kg the wetted surface was equal in either boat). The design incorporated many good ideas, with low wetted surface, right and left hull parts (instead of top and bottom) to permit a fine entry, and a low seat for stability. The new boat was offered to one of our best elite scullers, who was accustomed to rowing a (cigar-shaped) Empacher. He felt uncomfortable in the heavyweight Resolute, because – relative to the Empacher – it felt nervous and unstable. He elected to race the lightweight hull, which felt more like the Empacher. At his weight of 90kg, he lost all the advantage of reduced wetted surface. The relation did not last, and, sadly, the original Resolute single never went into extended production.

Note 3 – An exception is found on Graeme King's lovely wood singles, which offer certainly the best fin/boat setup for a windy, winding course. The fin is mounted well forward to resist drift without weather cocking. Mounted forward, it can be quite large without resisting intentional turns. The fin is raked aft to slide through sunken debris. King singles also have a pronounced banana shape, with a finely drawn bow and stern, as a further aid to easy turning.

Note 4 – the cited time difference on the Head Of The Charles course was derived from the number of strokes required to make a 45° turn. Each fin/boat combination was tested twice, in a confined turn space which required conformity between passes, and the results were averaged (in every case the difference was one stroke). The average number of strokes, to turn 45°, was applied to determine the degrees of turn in a single stroke, for each boat/fin combination. Then:

- ... Degrees of turn/stroke were divided into 413°, (the total arc of major turns on the Head Of The Charles course), to determine the number of turn strokes on the course.

- ... A nominal distance of 6.3 meters/turn stroke determined the distance covered while turning

- ... Distance used for turning was subtracted from the total distance of the Head Of The Charles, to give the distance rowed straight. The Head Of The Charles course is a little less than 4,650 meters, depending on the buoys. 4,650 meters was used for the calculation.

- ... A standard distance/stroke of 7.8 meters determined the number of strokes rowed straight.

- ... A stroke rate of 30 was applied for both turn and straight strokes, to determine the time spent turning and the time spent rowing straight. The two were added to determine total time on the course, for each boat/fin.

Note 5 – Most rowers would not agree, but a cut fin can also be faster in side-by-side races, except in strong crosswind conditions. Besides less skin drag, a small fin allows effortless, instant correction of course errors from inattention, boat wakes, or nicking a buoy. For boat wakes and eddies, where water is disturbed below the surface, a large fin does not help course keeping.

Note 6 – The Head of the Schuylkill is an exception. The river is wide and wind blowing down the river becomes a crosswind for the dogleg at Boathouse Row.

Note 7 - The term "stake turn" comes from 19th century professional match races. A great Thomas Eakins painting depicts the Biglin brothers "Turning at the Stake". In the painting, two stakes are marked with flags – blue for the Biglin brothers and red for their opponents, who are visible in the background, well behind.

Note 8 - Including Van Dusen, Carl Douglas, Hudson, Fluidesign, Filippi.

Oar Length and Rigging

Rigging for sprint races may be too heavy[1] for long distance. Rigging lighter loses a bit of distance on each stroke, but saves strength, and provides for easier acceleration. Accelerating quickly, to take the inside of a turn or to avoid another boat, can be vital in traffic situations.

Many rowers will lighten up for a head wind. Spacers, e.g. "Clams" from Concept 2, provide adjustment to pull the oar 1 cm inboard, giving more leverage and less effort.

> Even on a strong eight, clams can be applied for headwind conditions.

Every individual and crew is different. Oar blades and shafts vary. You can start with a "standard" set of dimensions[2], but only trials can tell what combination is best.

For head racing, trials should be over a fairly long distance (e.g. 2 km) at a comfortably fast pace, but not so fast that fatigue may influence the outcome, e.g. at stroke rate ±26 in a single. The difficulty is finding identical conditions for repeats. Consult the weather forecast to pick consecutive trial days. Fatigue may influence multiple trials on the same day.

Compare times over the set distance to determine the best rigging combination.

You may wish to hide the speed section of your SpeedCoach, to keep preconceptions from influencing the result.[3]

Test **one change** at a time, but understand that changing the spread will likely ask for a corresponding change to the inboard length of the oars.

A best oar length for one oar model may be dramatically different from the best length for another.

Oar flex is little understood. Some rowers insist that a stiff oar wastes the least energy, while other rowers prefer the whip action of a softer oar. As the boat accelerates on the pullthrough, rowers with a strong finish may keep the pressure on the blade constant, so that the oar stays bent all the way to release. For most of us, pressure on the blade is normally reduced by the boat's acceleration, so that the initial bend in the oar will tend to straighten out, returning the energy spent in bending it.

- Very strong rowers may not recover the initial cost of bending a soft oar, because they can keep it bent until released

- Less powerful rowers may recover the cost of bending the oar, as it whips straight during the pullthrough.

Just as lighter rigging may be better for head races, softer oar shafts may also be better, considering that less force can be applied over the length of a long course.

In sculling boats, oar comparisons are commonly done with Oar A on one side and Oar B on the other, then switching. This gives a feeling of how the two blades load up in the water, and how they hold their level, but does not really tell much about speed.

> For sweeps, trials are clearly complicated. The basic concept applies: repeated pieces over a set distance, with a set stroke rate. Coaches may need to fall back on opinion based on their research, or, simply, what oars are available.

Notes to Oar Length and Rigging

Note 1 – "Heavy" and "Light" refer to the load felt on the pullthrough. Rigging is well covered in rowing literature, and should be familiar to any coach. Except as applicable to racing over long distances, rigging is not in the province of this book. For rowers new to rigging, the following provides ranges for single sculls, and how the ranges relate to "heavy" and "light".

<u>Oar length</u>
from 289 cm (heavy) to 275 cm (light)

<u>Inboard length (from the oarlock to the handle tip)</u>
from 87 cm (heavy) to 90 cm (light) – can be adjusted quickly with a clam, available from the oar manufacturer

<u>Spread (the distance between the oarlock pins)</u>
from 159 cm (heavy) to 165 cm (light)

<u>Foot stretcher adjustment</u> has the effect of changing the spread – toward the stern (heavy) and toward the bow (light)

Individuals can row doubles with heavier rigging than singles, and quads with even heavier rigging. Generally, rigging for the crew should be the same, but variations in body size and shape may require individual adjustment, to match the arc of the oar paths. Matching oar paths is most easily advised by a coach with a view from outside the boat.

Note 2 – Many club boats and oars are rigged for elites, i.e. too heavy for beginning racers, and much too heavy for learning rowers.

Note 3 - Advice from Gregg Stone, from his test experience with his daughter Gevvie, presently USA's best woman sculler.

Weight

Within reasonable limits, using modern materials, and for the great majority of rowers, hull/rigger strength is no longer a concern for weight. Once upon a time, very light boats were destined for very short lives, no longer true.

FISA's weight minima are "daft" to use Carl Douglas' description, and widely ignored outside of elite competition. Few recent competitive singles weigh more than 14 kg, and rowers usually race their boat as delivered. Most boats winning head races weigh less than the FISA minima, but correlation does not mean causation, and the most probable reason is that most competitive boats in head races weigh less than the FISA minima.

Various sources provide opinions on the effect of weight on speed.

... lighter is necessarily better, because skin drag is reduced, or...

... because boat weight damps velocity variations (of the boat in the water and also of rower weight moving fore and aft in the boat) an ideal boat weight exists for any given rower weight (rower technique may influence the ideal boat weight, as well). A light boat can be slower than a heavier boat because the lighter boat's damping effect is insufficient. Heavier rowers will go faster in a heavier boat.[1]

In the 'lighter is better' camp, tank testing on a single, at a little less than 4 m/sec boat speed, shows a 0.27% increase in speed for a 1% reduction in weight.

On its website, Concept 2 projects boat speed in an eight, from erg times at given rower weights. Concept 2's formula shows a 0.25 % change in speed for a 1% change in weight in mid-range. The empirical result of the tank test and the Concept 2 figure correspond, although the eight moves much faster and – because skin drag increases exponentially by a factor of ^1.7, a greater effect would be expected.

Comparing winning race times of pairs and fours, with and without cox, shows a speed difference of 0.31%/1% of weight difference. These boats move faster than singles and the ratio corresponds to tank testing on the single at a speed of 5 m/sec. (If we could only sustain that speed in a single!)

For a kilo (2.2 lb) reduction in the static weight of boat and oars, we can estimate, from the preceding, about 2½ seconds saved in a race of 20 minutes. If motion damping is a factor, reducing boat weight may have less effect, or negative effect.

The biggest weight variable is the rower. In a single:

Rower	50 to 100 kg	Δ 50 kg
Boat & Oars	16 to 20 kg	Δ 4 kg
Total	66 to 120 kg	

If boat weight helps to damp velocity variations, the rower's motion fore and aft is the major factor that needs damping.

Naked single hulls weigh less than 7 kg. Accessories and oars account for over half of total boat weight. Titanium pins, lightweight shoes, smaller nuts and bolts, etc. can take weight out of a boat. Some oars are lighter than others. Seat pads (e.g. "Sorbothane") can be much heavier than necessary[2]. Multiple ways exist to reduce the weight of your boat, gain (maybe) a fraction in speed, and make it easier to carry.

Rower weight is worse than static weight.

Be lean

Notes to Weight

Note 1 – Rob Waddell's 2k World Record in the single was set in a 15.5 kg boat.

Note 2 – A low-cost light-weight seat pad (in fact, many pads) can be cut from a yoga mat, available in any big-box sports store.

Navigation

Learn the course

Pure boat speed is the most important factor for doing well. Next is steering the course. **The best course in a head race is no wider than the width of a boat**. Accurate navigation is a first priority.

It is astonishing that, after months of preparation and substantial cost, some competitors see a head race course for the first time while rowing to the start. Knowing the course means rowing it **before race day**.

> Coxes, despite their forward vision, are not exempt from the need for reconnaissance. From extended observation at Anderson bridge, the Eliot turn, and the Belmont Hill dock at the Head Of The Charles, **more coxes than scullers are likely to make steering errors.**[1]
>
> The cure for inexperience is studying the course. Coaches should include cox reconnaissance as part of their race preparation.

Ideally, match time of day and direction of tide to race conditions. Landmarks, course lines, and potential traps[2] should be committed to memory. A landmark should locate the start of your sprint, 40 to 50 strokes from the finish. Discussion with a coach and written notes, shortly after landing, reinforce memory.

Map study can provide insights that are not apparent on the water. The mind's eye tends to straighten out curves, but a map shows bends as they are, and helps to memorize features of the race course.

Following the course on land (e.g. by bicycle) and viewing the course from bridges can provide an extra perspective to round out the view from the water.

Resident racers are usually happy to share their knowledge. It is worth asking for advice.

Generalities about river current are worth remembering:

...   current flows fastest where the water is deepest – in the channel

...   typically, the channel and fastest current are on the outer side of a river bend, but there are many exceptions

Photo: Mason Cox

This aerial photo of the Charles River at Eliot Bridge shows its current's path to the outsides of the S-bend. Ice has melted faster over the current than over still water. Normally Charles River current is negligible, but can increase because of heavy rains, or – in this case – because of spring snowmelt.

If the channel is not obvious, the drift of floating leaves can often tell which part of the river moves fastest.

(Please see Appendix notes on London's Tideway, where staying in the channel is the main challenge of the race.)

In a fast flowing river, obstacles like bridge arches and shoreline irregularities can set up disturbing eddies. Shore-edge eddies can even flow upstream. Against a strong current, hugging the bank can be faster than rowing the rhumb line. To find out, do it both ways in practice, and record the time difference. Or row with another boat and compare.

A mirror saves time, in boats without a cox

Even when the course is so familiar that you could row it blindfolded, a mirror:

... can aim you straight between points, and minimize corrections

... eliminates body movements that disturb the boat

... anticipates converging situations with boats ahead

Some rowers with flexible necks say that they can pull as hard, while glancing over their shoulder, as they could with a mirror. This seems doubtful. Rowers who master the mirror don't revert.

Caveats apply:

... Some wide courses are so deprived of forward landmarks that the mirror gives little help for navigation. The only solution is familiarity with the correct perceived distance from the river banks.

... The mirror is like wearing blinders. Turning the head expands the mirror's scan. Areas to the side behind the shoulders, especially on the opposite side from the mirror, need to be checked directly and frequently.

... It is hard to judge distances with the mirror. One eye does not provide any depth perception.

... In wet weather, for rowers who wear glasses, rain can make vision difficult. A hat with a brim will keep rain off glasses. Some mirror users tuck the mirror under the brim of their hat, to shelter the mirror as well. A piece of cardboard or a piece of plastic can be taped above the mirror if it can't be sheltered under your hat's brim.[3]

Without a mirror, a visual check ahead is needed at least every fourth stroke, even when you are lined up on a landmark astern (in crosswinds or river current, holding a landmark dead astern will result in a curved course.) Tracking boats ahead is difficult without a mirror, and skirting boats, buoys and other obstacles needs a look ahead on almost every stroke,.

The time needed to master the mirror varies, but it is not overnight. Figure on three to six weeks of everyday use. Please refer to Appendix II - "Starting with the Mirror" for suggestions.[4]

Minimize turning

Rowing straight, all your energy is getting you to the finish line. In a turn, energy is wasted pushing bow and stern sideways, in opposite directions.

The shortest course looks like a series of lines between turns at bridge arches, points of land, or buoys, with the smallest possible radius for each turn.

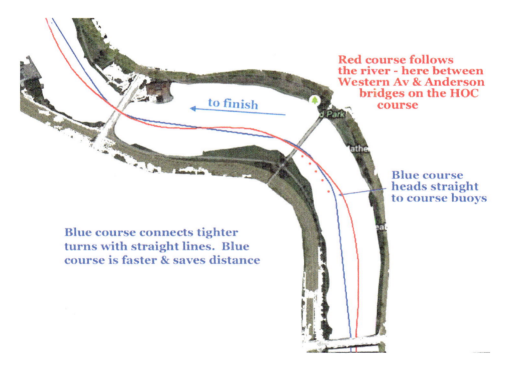

If buoys are arranged to lead racers around a bend, pick up the buoys where your straight course comes tangent to the line of buoys, then follow the buoys. But if the boat's speed (e.g. a fast eight) won't permit following the line of buoys, the cox must round out the turn (see p. 40).

Most river banks are not uniformly curved. If a long bend has small bends mixed with straight stretches, it's better to dig one or two hard turn strokes and row straight until another quick turn, than to match the long bend with continued pressure favoring one side.

Rowers can disagree on the best turn technique.[5] Most singles and doubles rowers can't describe what they do to turn, except to push on one leg (and some dispute which leg). **A short, quick stroke** has much to recommend it, although it breaks the good swing and glide established while rowing straight.

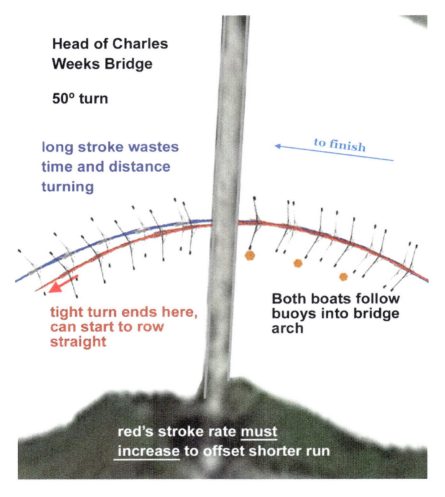

The red boat saves time and distance by getting through the turn sooner.

In a single, if the straight-line stroke rate is 28 or 29, the turning stroke rate should be at least 32 or 33, to compensate for the loss of distance per stroke. Higher stroke rates can actually increase speed. Greg Benning, a two-time HOC course record holder, describes his turns as 'like a racing start'.

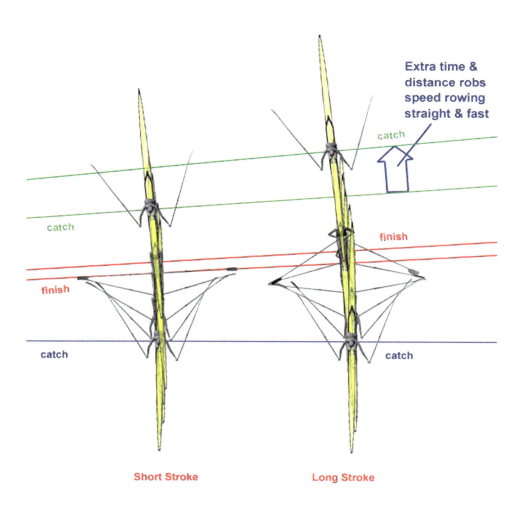

In this diagram, each stroke carries the right-hand boat further away from the curve of the course. The biggest difference is between the run of the two boats on the recovery.

Running straight between strokes takes you where you don't want to go. A short stroke permits a **quick recovery**, cuts time and run to the next catch, and tightens the arc of the turn.

The technique in a single or double:

... stretch the pulling arm beyond the normal catch position

... plant the blade deep, to bite at full stretch while the oar is 60° from perpendicular to the hull

... keep the pulling arm straight, push hard with your leg

... as soon as the pulling elbow starts to bend, release and go quickly for another stroke

The short stroke has other advantages. It:

... uses legs and glutes to move the bow sideways. Pulling past perpendicular gains little in turn angle, and pits weaker arms and shoulders against the fin, which resists moving sideways.

... keeps rower weight aft, to lift the bow and give the forward length of the boat less leverage to resist turning.

The oar on the inside of the turn does little except go through the pull-feather-pull motion, with no more pressure than needed to balance the boat.

Most rowers don't practice turning. A short, quick stroke requires a change of rhythm, and feels awkward if new. When changing course, even while paddling at a low stroke rate, consciously shortening up and raising the cadence can create a good reflex for head racing.[6]

Turning a big, fast boat is different.

A big, fast crew wants to turn quickly, but has other priorities –

... Cohesion of the entire crew, sustaining rhythm at high pressure

... Maintaining level set up, despite the destabilizing effect of hard steering,

In an elite eight, rowing at a rating of 35 or 36, the stroke rate is too high to raise it more.

Harvard, Northeastern, Boston University and MIT crews have the benefit of practicing turns each time they row on the Charles. Patrick Lapage at Harvard coaches a **long catch** for rowers on the inside of the turn, and a **long finish** for rowers outside the turn, maintaining stroke rate (35 or 36) and equal pressure on both sides. The long catch inside and long finish outside counteract the tendency of the boat to heel toward the outside of the turn. Equal pressure on both sides makes steering more predictable for the cox.

School, club, or masters crews that are not capable of sustaining high pressure at a high stroke rate may benefit from shortening the stroke and increasing stroke rate to reduce turning radius.

In his days as coach at MIT, Gordon Hamilton had his oarsmen reduce all inside pressure at the Weeks and Eliot turns on the Head Of The Charles course. He claims that his crews gained on these turns.

Published advice puts almost all the burden for turning on the cox. Herewith two examples that fall short of telling rowers how to get around a bend.

From CoxswaiNation/Yasmin Farooq

yaz@COXSWAINation.com. Link to:

http://www.coxswaination.com/KeysToSteeringEverySituation.pdf

"*Full tiller with possible assistance from your team. In head racing you often have to navigate some serious curves. For starters, your coach should review the course with the team and prepare everyone for strategizing for these turns. You will have to steer smoothly over several strokes, and may even need to "set the tiller" full port or full starboard. As you approach a major corner, let your team know it's coming up. Tell them when you begin to steer: "I'm starting the Weeks Bridge corner to port…I'm at full tiller,"* **Tell them if you plan to use their power: ("Starboards get ready to hit it…NOW"). If you need your other side to row with less pressure to make the turn, let them know** (emphasis provided). *As the turn is completed, tell the team when to return to "even pressure" and that you are straightening the boat out."*

Practice at home, before arriving at the race course, is omitted from this advice. Technique specifics are also lacking. The crew may understand "hit it" or "less pressure", but their comprehension is unlikely to have much effect.

From "The Short and Snarky Guide to Coxing and Rowing" – (at Amazon)

"<u>Steering Around Turns in Head Races or River Bends.</u> Steering around corners requires you to push the steering cords forward and hold them there (on both the drive and the recovery) for a few strokes or more. You obviously want to avoid over-steering, but sometimes the situation calls for bigger adjustments.

Ease the cords smoothly and steadily forward into the turn and hold it as far as it will go for as long as necessary. Then gradually ease the cords back to dead center at the top of the turn. Repeat as necessary.

Your rowers should be actively helping you move around the turn (e.g. by starboards lengthening out and ports shortening up). Let your rowers know that you will be steering and that they can expect to feel the rudder. You should warn your rowers in advance about turns, reminding them to adjust their length and power accordingly at critical times. If you are making big changes, keep them aware, but keep in mind that you should appear confident and matter-of-fact while doing so. If you make a big deal about a turn, indicate that you misjudged, or otherwise hesitate, they will lose confidence in you and will not navigate the turn well. If you normally row on a straight course, make sure you are practicing turns before head racing at other venues. "

"Make sure you are practicing turns before head racing" is golden counsel – specific turning technique is needed as well.

For head racing, turning technique must be coached and practiced, before race day.

Start turning **NOW**

Turning at the right moment seems so obvious that it shouldn't be worth mentioning. But in the heat of battle, it is easy to focus on other things - while the moment flashes by. When the moment comes to turn, do it.

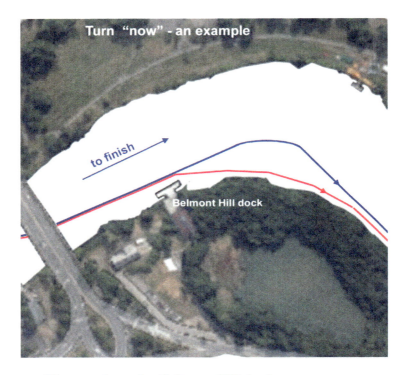

The turn is at the Belmont Hill dock - The blue course missed the turn - this is the 2nd most missed turn at the Head of the Charles (after the turn under Anderson bridge)

At the Head Of The Charles, dozens of boats (or hundreds; please see course notes in the Appendix) go too far before starting to turn here. Pay attention to where you are. Start turning the moment you can.

Risk vs Reward

Safe is faster than sorry. Advisory buoys have a reason, like a sunken log or rock. Hitting a bridge by turning too close is slow.

A classic risk-reward question is posed by the infamous Eliot bend at the Head Of The Charles. The course turns almost 170°, over a distance of 840 meters. The question is: should the port blade be inside the course buoys, or outside? Putting the buoys under the oarlock reduces the radius of the turn by ± 1.5 meters.

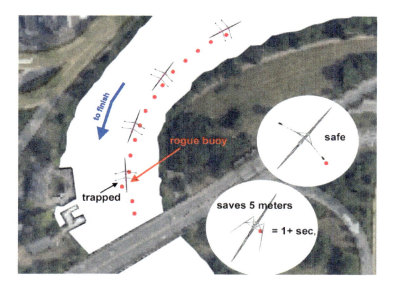

Rowing close to but outside the buoys adds about 5 meters to the distance rowed, or a little more than a second at 4 meters/second. If the buoys on the turn were perfectly placed, putting the port oarlock over the buoys might be worth a second. But buoys can be misplaced and can move during a regatta. A rogue buoy can easily sit 2 or 3 meters out of line, and rogue buoys can be difficult to see (or impossible, when sun glare intervenes at the beginning or end of the day).[7]

The gain is not worth the risk of a penalty from cutting a buoy.

A confession: with perfect visibility - no sun glare or rain - **and** if the buoys were still in line when setting out for the start – need to check – I put my port oarlock over the buoys. But perfect conditions are not usual.

> **For a fast-moving eight**, the arc in the Eliot turn's last meters is too tight to follow. The best course is to let the buoys fall away before the arc gets tight, and round out the turn.

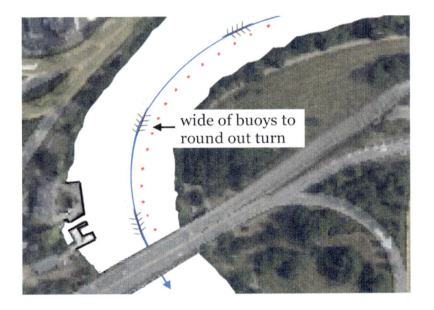

> **Don't let the line of turn buoys get away from you.** If another boat is on the inside of the turn, stay close abeam. Call to the inside boat's cox if the inside boat is pushing you too far out: "MAKE THE TURN" or similar.

Notes to Navigation

Note 1 – 1,200 coxes steered boats up the river at the Head Of The Charles in 2014, compared to 1,000 scullers.

Note 2 – a sure course record at the Head Of The Charles was spoiled by a low-hanging branch on the last bend before the finish. The racer, a local, was familiar with the course, but didn't note this particular hazard, and it cost not only the record but two places in the results. Ugh.

Note 3 – Richard Kendall relates: "Don McSween & I rowed the Housatonic on a rainy day. Ale-choholic that I am, I cut an extended visor out of a Yuengling six pack and duct taped it to Don's hat mirror. XXXX derided us with mocking humor. Don proceeded to win the 1x while XXXX received 8 buoy penalties." (redacted, to spare the buoy cutter)

Note 4 – Hyndsight® (www.hyndsightvision.com) offers a camera mounted forward of the rower, with a screen mounted above the stretcher. It is not yet possible to assess its usefulness. One early user reports that it is helpful but doesn't replace the mirror.

Note 5 - Rowers in disagreement include my wife. Her stroke is long and fluid, sustaining speed at a low rating. She says to turn "even". Her course record at the Head Of The Charles suggests that her method makes up in speed, for her, what it may lose in added distance.

Note 6 - Many rowing venues are confined to long straights with no natural turns. It may look odd to zigzag down a straight body of water, but it's better than learning to turn in a race. The best drill for turning is slaloming between moored boats in a harbor, but not all rowers/crews have the opportunity.

Note 7 – For events late in the day at twilight, buoys hidden by darkness can't be seen by an umpire on the shore, any better than they can be seen from a boat. But it's not worth taking a chance.

Traffic

Seeding and the Broken Accordion

Head race organizers try to start faster boats ahead of slower boats. Results in the preceding year are commonly used to seed an event. In principle, the fleet going up the river will expand like an opening accordion.

This tends to work for the first boats to start. Also, faster rowers have more experience for staying on course and out of trouble. Passing situations are less common, and are usually resolved without issues.

The accordion doesn't work in the back half, because:

... With no precedent to sort fastest from slowest, slower boats start ahead of faster boats. Passing situations are common, and often involve more than two boats

... Rowers and coxes in the back half tend to be less experienced and less familiar with the course. They are more likely to make mistakes that involve other boats.

Examples cited below are all drawn from personal experience, with the benefit of perfect hindsight. They are only examples. Every head race is rich with new experiences, and no text could anticipate every traffic situation.

Instead, the following is intended to stimulate awareness, most especially for back starters who are new to head racing. The selected scenarios are intended to provoke mental readiness for any contingency, a big step toward overcoming the handicap of inexperience.

Common sense wins over rules – no matter who has the right of way, a collision is slow for all parties. Unfortunately, common sense is sometimes forgotten in the heat of competition.

Passing

A passing boat should choose the inside of a bend (but please see discussion below on "S" bends). Adequate space without oar banging requires ±6 meters separation between the hulls of sculling boats, 7 meters between fours and eights.

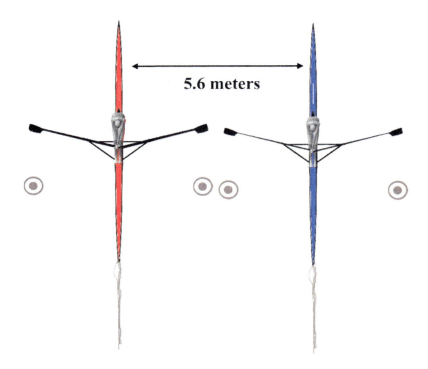

With 5.6 meters separation between sculling boats, the difference between the inside and the outside of a bend is significant – at the Head Of The Charles, for the Eliot bend, it is roughly 4 seconds, and for the big bend from the Belmont Hill Dock to the finish, it is roughly 2 seconds. The equivalent distance is 32 meters for 4 seconds, and 16 meters for 2 seconds. While stuck on the outside of a bend, making up this much distance is tough. Passing clear ahead from the outside is unlikely, unless there is a serious mismatch between the two boats.

Even on the river Po, which looks relatively straight to the eye, a boat trying to pass upstream on the outside of the long arc at mid-course will have great difficulty getting ahead of a slower boat.

Taking the Inside

Stopping is not what any racer wants. If a turn is coming up, it is far better to **accelerate to take the inside** from in front of a slower boat. But situations arise where you can't get clear ahead. In a single or double, **stopping** briefly will get to the finish line faster than hanging on the outside, all the way around the bend.

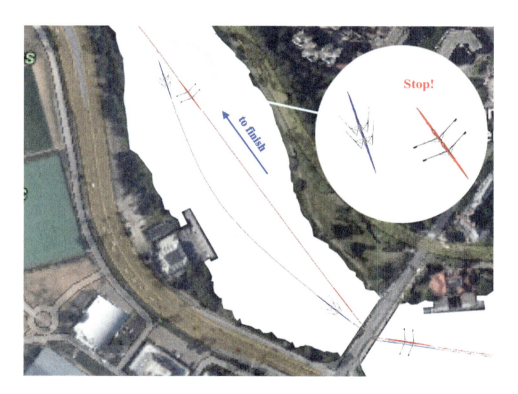

In the illustration above, the red boat is rowing faster than the blue boat, and follows it under the bridge. Under the bridge, the blue boat makes an insufficient turn upstream. The red boat, rowing faster on a shorter course, converges as the two boats arrive at the start of the Eliot bend.

The red boat will get to the finish line faster if it stops, to cut behind the blue boat and take the inside of the turn.[1]

For eights, fours, or quads, it does not make sense to stop.

Waiting for a 17-meter eight takes longer than waiting to tuck behind an 8-meter single.[2] At 5.2 m/sec instead of 4 m/sec, seconds lost on the outside of the turn are less. And, a break in rhythm is harder to recover for four or eight rowers. Better to row around the turn outside the slower boat.

If the red eight's cox is alert to the situation coming out of Anderson Bridge, she can tell the crew to go hard for the next turn, and call a Power-10, or two. Over the next 50 strokes, red's crew needs to gain an extra length to win the inside of the Eliot turn, as seen in the following diagram.

Red has won the inside of the Eliot turn ahead. This is an intelligent use of ATP-CP. Blue boat must follow in red's wake.

If you are ahead of a faster boat, steer early to stay clear. If you are being overtaken, you must give the overtaking boat freedom to clear on the side of her choice. Too many novice racers freeze on their line, blocking rowers coming up astern. Steer to stay clear.

As soon as you see that you will be overtaken, try to be smart about where and when. By getting off the preferred line early, you can make the passer's choice obvious - better for the passing boat, and better for you. If a turn is coming up, take the outside early. Let the passing boat go by quickly and tuck back in on the best line.

Coxes have the advantage of forward vision, but they can't see well behind. Stroke oars in eights and stern-coxed fours, and bow oars in bow-loaded fours, must tell the cox what is happening astern. Rules of the Head Of The Charles spell out the need. Here is an excerpt:

For boats being passed – *"Communicate effectively during racing. All shells with bow-loaded coxswains are strongly advised to have their bow seat rower notify the coxswain if a following crew is about to make a pass and on which side the passer is approaching. Timely instruction from the bow seat rower may assist the coxswain in avoiding an interference penalty."*

For boats passing – *"Communicate effectively during racing. All shells with bow-loaded coxswains are strongly advise to have their bow seat notify the coxswain when there is clear water astern after completing the pass. Timely instruction from the bow seat rower may assist the Passer's coxswain in avoiding stern-to-bow collision and/or an interference penalty due to cutting in too soon."*

(Full rules are included in the Head of the Charles section, Appendix Course Notes)

Don't race a passing boat. Your max sustainable pace is the pace to hold, to get to the finish line in the best time. The faster a passer goes by, the sooner you will be clear to navigate the best course.

If a boat has caught you, and you are rowing at your max sustainable pace, it means one of two things:

...   the other boat is being pushed at an unsustainable pace. If that is true, you will likely row it down as you approach the finish.

...   the other boat is simply faster

Either reason should not change your race plan. Holding off the passer is a mistake.

... holding off the passer

A futile effort to stay ahead is likely to induce burnout, while still far from home.

just 300 more strokes to the finish...

"S" bends are rare, and they present a challenge. In the following illustration, red is catching up with blue at "1".

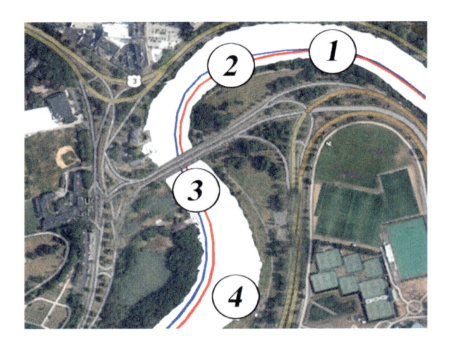

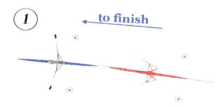

At "1" red has a choice to take the inside of the bend or to follow blue...

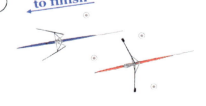

Blue goes wide to make room for red, and red takes the inside...

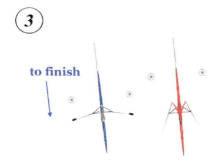

Coming out of the bridge arch, red has not passed blue, and the course will soon turn the other way.

At "4" red is stuck on the outside of the next turn. Red can stop (costs 2 seconds) and tuck in behind blue, but can only make up 2 seconds by rowing on the inside of the turn, with no net gain.

Red's choice at "2" was a mistake.

A better course for red is shown here:

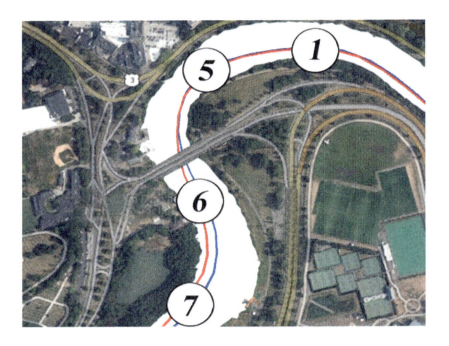

Red estimates that too little distance remains before the end of the turn, to pass clear ahead of blue.

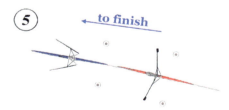

Instead of taking the space offered by blue, red follows blue around the turn, slowing down just enough to keep clear.

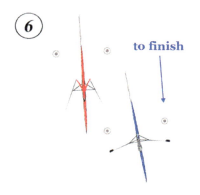

Coming under the bridge, red moves up at "6" to take the inside of the next turn. Blue must yield room for red to pass.

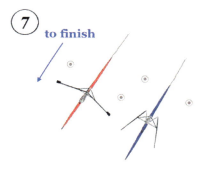

At "7" red is comfortably on the inside. Red will pass blue easily before the finish, and finish in less time.

If you commit to pass on the first bend of an "S" curve, you **must complete the pass before you arrive at the next bend**. The effort can be another use for ATP-CP. If you aren't sure you can pass clear ahead by the end of the first bend, the second course shown above is better.

> **Should big boats hang back** on the first part of an S-bend, to take the inside instead of being hung out to dry on the last part of the S? If crew and coxswain are capable of adjusting, it seems like a good idea.

Avoiding Contact

Ticking blade against blade is not recommended, but oar banging is not a collision. If oars clash, the faster boat should **KEEP ROWING**. Both boats can turn away if there is room, or the slower boat can stop. If both boats stop, the misery continues. **KEEP ROWING**.

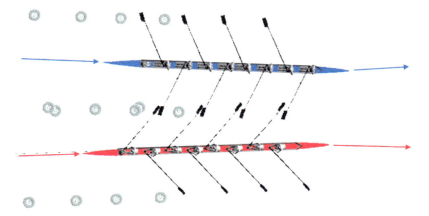

In the diagram above, a gentle steer is enough to row clear. Converging contact is not interference, if neither boat is passing and both are approximately on course. It is part of head racing.

The following situation is similar to the preceding, but the boats have converged beyond mere oar banging.

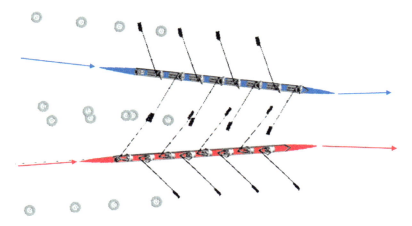

Inside oars should **keep rowing** as long as blades are clear of the other hull. With outside oars idle and coxes steering, the two boats will pull away from each other.

Red's cox must call "Starboard way enough," and Blue's cox must call "Port way enough." Both coxes steer to stay clear.

If both sides of both boats <u>keep</u> rowing, the two boats will collide.

If both sides of both boats <u>stop</u> rowing, the two boats will collide.

Passing other boats should be easy, if they get out of the way. What if they don't? Safety and common sense come first. **Never row into a collision**.

Be wary of boats ahead that are off course. More than one errant boat has been T-boned while turning into the path of faster boats coming up behind. In the illustration below, blue is off the line into the bridge arch, while red is coming up fast. Blue should give room for red to pass.

BUT red should be prepared for blue to wrongly turn back toward the arch...

Red's cox can hail blue, "EIGHT AHEAD – GIVE WAY" – but blue is unlikely to respond. It is already late for red to take action.

Red must stop. It's blue's fault (blue may be penalized for interference), but that doesn't help red's time.

Red should have steered early to avoid blue, even though blue is in the wrong place.

Avoiding collisions is important for all boats, and especially for big boats. Compared to singles or doubles, the risk of injury or serious damage is greater. Seconds fly by while disentangling long hulls and intermeshed oars.

"Way Enough", called early to avoid a collision, **costs less time and energy than a panic "Hold All"**.

A stopped crew should be ready to row **before "ready all"**. The most stable position puts hands past knees toward the stern, with knees flexed. But any position with oars feathered is good, if each rower knows it. Practice beforehand helps.

"READY ALL ROW!" may come out as one command if the cox is in a hurry to start rowing. If each rower is ready, the first stroke will be in unison, and the next 4 or 5 strokes can be like a mini racing start.

ready for "READY..."

If the crew is not in position **before** "READY ALL ROW", the first 4 or 5 strokes will be spent getting the crew together.

not ready for "Ready..."

Be prepared to shift gears mentally

The preceding examples don't begin to describe the infinite variety of traffic situations that arise in a head race. Shifting focus is hard for many aggressive rowers and coxswains, who instinctively ignore other boats and try to will their way through, hoping for luck when reality demands anticipation and response.

When other boats are in the way, boat speed and the ideal course become secondary. The first priority in close traffic is to find the best way: accelerating, steering around, slowing down, or even stopping. Once clear, you can shift gears back into speed mode.

Adjusting for other boats' mistakes is not agreeable, but may be the fastest way to the finish.

Collisions

As a sport, rowing extols teamwork. In a collision where two boats are locked together, **the most important part of the team is in the other boat**. Both boats must cooperate, to get separated and on their way.

... recriminations do not help.

You can't train for collisions. It's impossible to develop good reflexes that guarantee effective movements. **Your brain has to be put in charge.**

Boats can be separated by **pushing** or by **rowing**, or by a combination of the two. It may not be immediately clear which to do, or in what sequence.

... give your mind a second to digest the problem, and then, neither frozen nor frenzied, act with deliberate speed.

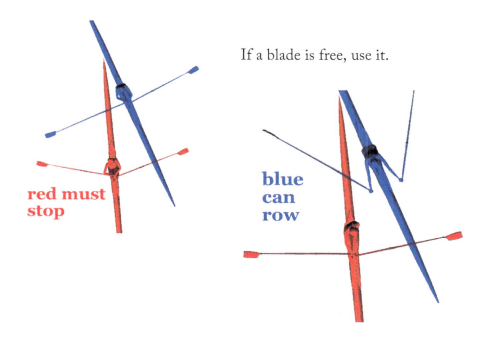

If a blade is free, use it.

red must stop

blue can row

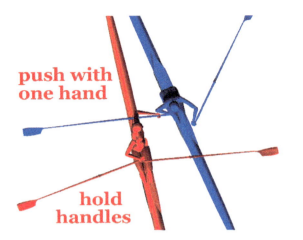

If a rigger or an oar's blade or shaft from the other boat is within reach, push it away.

If your oar is being pushed, grip it so that it doesn't move.

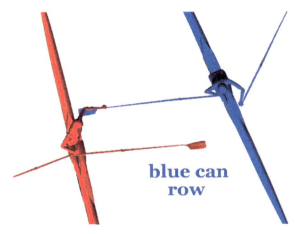

The situation on the following page appears desperate. Blue is wedged between red and a bridge piling, and unable to row. Red can't row ahead without pushing its bow into blue.

Neither blue nor red can reach an oar from the other boat, to push away.

nothing to push & no way to row

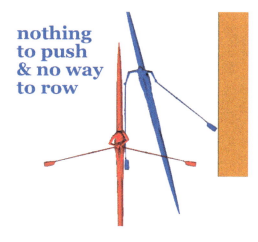

Red's port oar is free. Red can back away to come unglued from blue.

When backing with one oar, the hull pivots around the fin to turn in a tight arc.

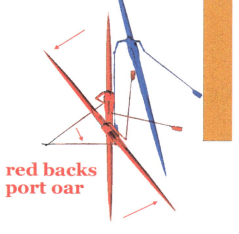

red backs port oar

blue can shove off

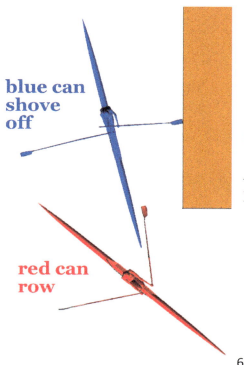

Remember to stay upright.

Avoid collisions, but be prepared.

red can row

photo: Peter Spurrier

... are you prepared for this?

Notes to Traffic

Note 1 – Nobody is going to use a calculator while on the race course, but it may help to have an idea of the mathematics involved. On the Eliot turn (840 meters, 170°), for a single scull rowing at 4m/sec, 2 seconds lost while stopping to take the inside will result in a net 2 second gain by the Belmont Hill dock, because the inside of the Eliot turn is worth about 4 seconds.

In a single, stopping abreast and coasting until clear loses a boat length, or 8 meters (8 meters / 4 meters/second = 2 seconds). Some energy will be recaptured for a fast restart, and the stop may not even lose 2 seconds on the course.

Note 2 – The following table shows the difference between an eight and a single, calculating seconds gained by stopping abeam to take the inside of the Eliot bend.

	Eight – 17m	Single – 8m
Distance between boats	7m	5.6m (dist. is added to radius)
Added distance on outside of turn	20.5m	16.4m
Added time if outside of turn	4.0 sec's @ 5.2m/sec	4.1 sec's @ 4m/sec
Wait time stopped	3.3 sec's @ 5.2m/sec	2.0 sec's @ 4m/sec
Net gain at finish	0.7 sec's	2.1 sec's

For ¾ second difference (= 3.5m) it is not worth disrupting eight rowers by stopping and restarting when boats are abeam. If a faster eight is clearly behind while converging from the outside, it may make sense to ease pressure and steer to tuck in behind the slower boat, to take the inside of the bend.

Training for Long Distance

A good coach is essential, not only for technique, but also to keep your aerobic training in balance with high intensity training.

... "Power" is energy produced per unit of time. As used here, "power" follows common usage, to mean peak power over a brief time, in the same way that we refer to an engine's horsepower.

Unfortunately, many rowers and some coaches have a 'more is more' philosophy. They imagine that peak power is the key to winning races. Competitive spirits enjoy going out each day to conquer, and don't feel good unless their bodies feel bad.[1]

"No pain no gain," has its place, but not every day. An intensity overload is counter-productive for head races.

Most of the wisdom for straight-line racing applies equally for head races. Tudor Bompa's "Theory and Methodology of Training" is a standard reference.[2] Ed McNeely's "Training for Rowing" is excellent. Jan Olbrecht's "The Science of Winning", a guide for swimmers, expresses the difficulty of developing power without sacrificing endurance.

The essential lesson is that endurance takes a long time to build. Power, by contrast, can be developed more quickly, but at the expense of endurance. Balancing the two is the key to effective training for head racing.

For head races, **endurance (i.e. sustained power) is more important than peak power**. Building endurance requires a long lead time. Ideally, training for a head race in November should begin not later than January.

As a rule of thumb – courtesy of Guenter Beutter at GMS – time spent at AT and above should be no more than 10% over the year. It's educational to keep a log and track the percentage. Individual tolerance for intense exercise varies, but from personal experience, and comparing with training plans that have proven effective, time spent at AT and above should increase to ± 15% in the weeks preceding an important race. More than 20% is likely to diminish endurance.

From a study of elite athletes, Stephen Seiler, a Norwegian scientist and rower, cites 80-20 as the typical balance of time spent between low intensity and high intensity exercise, with questionable benefits at the upper end of the high intensity scale.[3]

... Some authorities (Volker Nolte et al.) have correctly noted that the sequence of sprint races in the spring and summer, with head races in the fall, is the opposite of ideal. It would be better to build endurance for head races, and to build peak power after head racing is done.

... For racers who participate in summertime sprint races, especially in August or early September, recovery with extended aerobic retraining is helpful in the weeks preceding fall head racing. The goal is to rebuild endurance even at the expense of losing power.

The following page is intended to show emphasis on aerobic training. It is a graphic rendering of a training log, for twelve months ending in November 2014, Silverskiff-to-Silverskiff. The bars on the right show the division of weekly minutes between aerobic exercise and intense exercise (AT and above). The green bars on the left indicate minutes in the gym on strength training.

"Aerobic Exercise", in blue, represents 89.8% of minutes excluding gym time. Although blue bars dominate all through the year, the ratio of aerobic vs intense exercise changes according to the race schedule.

The chart is **not intended as a training model**. Individuals have different training needs and responses.

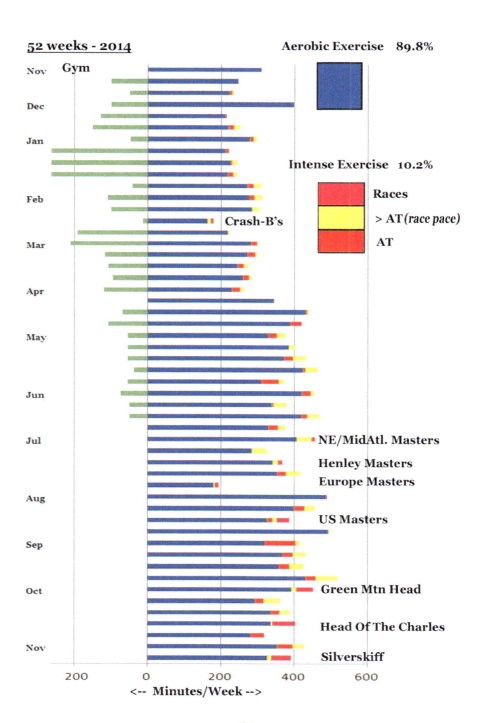

In the chart:

- Gym work stopped soon after the first half of the year. (See Appendix I on questions about Strength Training)

- Even leading up to Crash-B's and summer sprint races, high intensity time was **less than 15% of total**.

- 1k sprints at European Masters and US Masters Nationals were both followed by **a recovery week devoted to long aerobic workouts.**

- AT pieces started two weeks after US Masters and were gradually replaced by hi-intensity pieces at race pace (above AT) until the first head race, Green Mountain Head, six weeks later.[4]

Many racers follow a long range plan, and good models exist (e.g. Tudor Bompa's macro and micro cycles). Because of work and family needs, travel days, and weather issues, it can be hard to follow a strict plan over a period of months. The chart above is an actual record, not theoretical. It shows that a logical progression, with an ebb and flow of aerobic exercise, is possible without a long range plan. Instead of long range planning, it can be useful to plan workouts a few weeks in advance of major competitions, to be sure of achieving a good balance.

Above all, follow Gregg Stone's recommendation, "at a master's level, I recommend that people allow themselves to practice in the way that they enjoy most. If you are enjoying rowing you will do more and take more hard strokes. I would much rather go out with others and have some fun. Racing is only a small part of the rowing experience." Only a few rowers find self-fulfillment in misery. For most of us, training should be fun.

Tapering before an important race is customary, to be rested and ready after building power for the race. Because head race preparation involves less intense exercise than preparation for sprints, the taper period can be shorter. Individuals vary. Many experienced racers like to do a head race one week before the Head Of The Charles. I prefer a 6-kilometer piece six or seven days before the Head Of The Charles – the extra distance seems to have a psychological benefit. During the remaining days before the target race, brief high-intensity intervals keep neural paths prepared for a racing stroke rate.

Physiology is mostly genetic, although we can influence our shape by how we eat and how we train. Sprint races favor rowers with muscle mass. Weight training to build (or just keep) muscle mass is probably helpful, especially after age 50, but less probably useful within the last three months before a head race.

... Long races favor David over Goliath. In 2005 Steve Tucker (145 lbs) set a record at the 9.4 km Armada Cup, and since then only one racer has rowed the race faster. Andrew Campbell (155 lbs) set a new record at the 2014 Head Of The Charles, against world-class heavyweight competition.

... At the upper end of the age scale, my friend and rowing opponent, Henry Hamilton, is 25+ lbs lighter than myself. I have not beaten his time at the Head Of The Charles or Silverskiff since 2007. But in 1k sprint races he has never been able to beat me, because my size helps in a sprint.

The disparity between sprint and head race performance most likely comes from the cardio-vascular system's delivery capacity, relative to the muscles it must feed. The cardio-vascular system supplies oxygen to the muscles. It is mostly on or near the body's surface. Skinny muscles have more surface than bulky muscles, relative to their mass (they are, literally, "skin-ny").

In a short race, bulk can win, but the demands of a long race put more importance on oxygen delivery, and skinny wins. The same can be said for muscular smaller rowers: overall they have more skin, relative to their muscle mass, than bigger rowers. For that reason, small rowers do better in long races.

Separate medals for lightweights make no sense in head races. Many top head races have seen elite lightweights win overall. Their oxygen delivery advantage offsets any power deficit.

Age is the enemy of speed, in every sport. Happily for elder head racers, age deterioration is less for head racing than for sprints.

Around the world, systems to equalize ages have been based on sprint race results, extrapolated to longer distances. This has exaggerated the "handicap" advantage given to elder racers in head races, by a factor of 25% to 30%. Racers who compete in races with age adjustments can feel good about getting older – unlike most aspects of ageing.

At the Head Of The Charles, in a six-year study, speed of the men in the 50-59 age group declined at a greater rate than the decline in the 60-69 group. Why? Because the 50-59 group has more strength to lose; the 60-69 group has lost most of its muscle, and efficient technique has become more important.[5] Faster racers lose more with age than slower racers –because faster racers start with more strength and have more to lose as they age.

From age 40 to age 80, most speed-endurance sports show a steady downward slope in performance. The ski-jump profile in head racing, with a sharper decline in the 50's and leveling from 60 on to 80 [2], is not seen in swimming, running, bicycling, or triathlon. Even on the indoor rowing ergometer, times show steadily increasing attrition with age. The difference between rowing on water and other speed sports is the greater importance of efficient technique – rowing well offsets loss of power. Other sports certainly require efficient technique, but to a much lesser degree.

Two lessons to draw from these observations are that...

1. **Efficient technique is vital** at any age. Technique can always be improved, and can be lost as well.

Coaching can't be over-emphasized. A coach with a practised eye is needed, not every day but certainly every month, to gain (or retain) the most boat speed with the least wasted effort.

2. **Lean is good and bulk is slow**. A lean physique will get you to the finish faster in a long race. Diet can make a difference, and many diets have passionate advocates. For well-informed common sense advice on nutrition, refer to Nancy Clark's book, "Sports Nutrition Guidebook", but don't follow her "bulk up" advice unless you are way too thin.

As a final word on training for head racing, opinions differ on the value of vitamin supplements. Readers who are interested in vitamins might refer to Kenneth Cooper's "The Anti-Oxidant Revolution", published over thirty years ago and still a valuable reference.[6] I follow his vitamin recommendation for 'distress exercise'. It seems to do no harm, and may do some good.

Notes to Training, Physiology, and Age

Note 1 – For many years, "more is more" was the prevailing philosophy, as recorded accurately in the great book, "The Boys in the Boat". Technique was secondary to work, and the coach's main job was not to teach technique (which in any case was not well understood) but to find the best combination of workers. Luck was a major factor in finding the right combination, while the "boys" were beating each others' brains out. Sometimes it was successful, e.g. The Boys in the Boat at the 1936 Olympics, although other USA crews did not fare as well, then or since.

During the 70's, primarily in the East Bloc, science was applied to endurance sports, and ideas changed. Today, elite training involves high intensity work and a lot of it, but always on top of a strong aerobic base. See Note 3 below.

Note 2 - Tudor Bompa's "Periodization of Strength" is aimed at lifters, not rowers, and is not pertinent for rowing.

Note 3 - For a scientific view on endurance training for rowers, a Google search on "Stephen Seiler" will produce an abundance of in-depth commentary, with extensive references to other scientific research. The 80-20 low intensity-high intensity balance comes from "The Role of Intensity and Duration in Endurance Training". Stephen Seiler is a former rower based at the University of Agder, in Kristiansand, Norway.

Note 4 – Sharp eyes may see a disconnect between races rowed "at AT" and training rows "at AT" as opposed to "> AT" or "race pace". Indeed long races are rowed on the high end of AT, where oxygen delivered by the cardio-vascular system is sufficient to offset glycolysis and "the burn".

As used here, "AT" is defined as 4mMol of lactate – last measured for myself at HR 155 – this corresponds to a stroke rate 2 or 3 beats off my race pace, with HR into the mid 160's at the end of a long piece. ">AT" or "race pace" is at racing stroke rates, with HR going into the 170's, up to 180, as in a race. (Younger rowers can add 30 or 40 bpm to my HR values.)

Note 5 – in 2012, Head Of The Charles events for single rowers age 60+ were split into 5-year age groups, following the divisions established by FISA (the international governing body for rowing). The change at the Head Of The Charles eliminated and replaced 10-year groups that had age adjustments.

Three quarters of elder head racers who were polled at the time regretted doubling the number of medals. Even so, a strong argument can be made for the change, to spread joy among twice as many people.

Given that FISA 5-year age divisions are now part of the system at the Head Of The Charles, excluding the 50-59 group is totally loony.

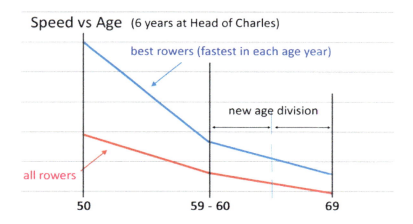

The 50 to 59 group loses speed at a greater rate than older rowers and should be split into two divisions, as now done for the 60-69's. Or apply an age adjustment.

Note 6 - Dr Cooper claimed part responsibility for declining heart disease mortality during the past decades, because he promoted the value of exercise to protect against heart attacks. He was the first to use the term "aerobics". His friends included many elite long distance runners. Some suffered from ailments that Dr Cooper attributed to an excess of free radicals (oxidants) caused by intense effort, and a few of his athletes died young, inspiring him to write the book.

Meta-analysis of multiple studies has suggested that vitamin supplements may do more harm than good, perhaps by diminishing the body's ability to synthesize vitamins from natural sources (e.g. vegetables). The meta-analysis seems to have been focused on vitamin therapy for illness. The analysis does not appear to have included studies of vitamin supplement use to counter the cascade of free radicals that follows intense exercise.

Race Preparation

Every head race teaches lessons. The following notions are a grab bag.

... The day before, do as much as you can to attach shirt and bow numbers, make equipment checks, and arrange transportation. A checklist and a timetable are both useful.

... Do not change your boat's rigging just before racing.

... With borrowed or rented equipment, apply your own rigging measures, but beware. Seat height varies above the waterline, and the difference can change the ideal height of pins above the seat. Foot stretchers vary in angle and minimum height. Row and adjust before race day.

... Follow your habitual routine in the days and hours before the race. Don't do anything that might upset your body clock or digestion. Plan a normal evening meal and early bedtime.

... Regattas are an occasion for seeing old friends. Socializing is good, but better after racing than before.

... Mentally row the course the night before, trying to remember each turn and imagining traffic situations. Practice calamities in your head, to be ready on the water.

... Allow adequate time after eating before racing. Two hours seems like a minimum.

... Eat a good breakfast, with a balance of fat, protein, and low-glycemic carbs. (Combined with the preceding, a very early wakeup call may be needed for an early morning race.)

- Warm up before going on the water. Ten easy minutes on an erg, enough to work up a sweat, is ideal. Especially on cold mornings late in the fall, the first minutes on the water can be chilling. Offset the cold by warming up beforehand.

- A warmup overgarment is customary; be sure that it's easy to remove and stow before the start.

- Individuals have widely varied tolerance for cold, and dress accordingly for racing. Some racers are comfortable in a tank top at 40°F. Being overdressed can cost energy for heat dispersion, but a greater risk is rowing too cold. Cold muscles can't work hard. I want to be sweating hot, even after waiting awhile to be called up for the start. On a cold day, that means a couple of upper layers, and tights.

- For temperatures near freezing, especially if it is windy, a hat conserves body heat. Rowing with gloves is better than rowing with numb fingers (baseball batting gloves fit snugly and stop wind chill).

- If it is very cold, feet can be kept warm by draping a piece of polar fleece over shoes. Even a towel can make a big difference. (I row with foot straps instead of shoes – foot straps allow super thick socks, warmer than any shoe-sock combination.)

- Start hydrating before rowing, and take fluid with you. A 50-50 blend of water and a sports drink (GatorAde®, PowerAde®, etc.) is better than just water or just sports drink. Keep hydrating on the way to the start, even if the weather is cold and you don't feel thirsty. Over-hydration is theoretically possible, but unlikely in pre-race conditions.

- Gu® or Hammergel®, following the instructions on the packets, go quickly into the system, and seem to promote endurance.

Summing up

Add the bits:	Time gained for a single scull, in a 20 minute race
1 kg (2.2 lbs) out of the boat & oars, ignoring any damping effect	2½ seconds (maybe)
2.3 kg (5 lbs) out of rower weight	5½ seconds
An easy turning fin instead of stock	5+ seconds
Steering to row 4660 meters instead of 4850 meters	49 seconds
No collisions and no penalties	no gain, but no loss!
	62 seconds

62 seconds is the difference between winning and missing the 5% cut for a guaranteed entry, in the following year's Head Of The Charles.

Rowing fast is primary, but the factors noted here have nothing to do with simply rowing fast. Steering is by far the most important of these. Rowing fast is not enough.

The title of this book is "Winning Head Races". Few rowers can finish first in every race, but most can improve versus competition without rowing noticeably faster. First or forty-first, every race rowed well is a victory, especially if it is better than the last.

Appendix I – Strength Training

Folklore:-- Doctors prescribed antibiotics to cure a boy's ailment. His doting grandmother prescribed chicken soup. The boy got well. Answering suggestions that medicine had cured the boy, grandma said, "well, chicken soup didn't hurt."

It's about the same story for strength training ("resistance training"). The best you can say is "strength training didn't hurt." But the only studies to support this are based on beginner rowers. We could benefit from a controlled study with trained, technically proficient rowers, but if such a study was ever done, it would probably look at 2k performance and not be predictive for long distance results.

My own experience is inconclusive, comparing seasons with strength training late in the year versus others with little or no gym time. I don't know:

1) whether resistance training increases speed over long distance.

2) what kind of resistance training is most effective.

All serious sources, on line and in print, agree that resistance training should relate to movements used in the sport. "Sport specific" is a common refrain. Training neural triggers, which put muscles to work, is as important as building the muscles themselves.

Stephen Seiler (a Norwegian rower/scientist; search on "Stephen Seiler") emphasizes that muscle size needs to be matched with aerobic capacity to retain endurance. Muscle bulk risks mitochondrial dilution and loads the oxygen delivery system.

... For rowing resistance training, Seiler recommends bungee rows. Bungee rows can be replicated on the erg at damper setting "8" up to "10". On water or on the erg, I do 1-minute intervals with 1-minute rest, at a stroke rate of 18 or less. This is 'sport specific' but neural triggers may adapt adversely to the low stroke rate. To conclude a bungee row, 1-minute high stroke intervals without the bungee may be useful as correction.

In the winter and spring, for many years and still today, I visit a gym two to three times a week In summer and fall, much less or not at all. Does mid-year rowing retain the strength gained in the winter? Maybe some, and certainly not all.   One excellent elite sculler continues circuit training in a gym until two or three days before major competition.

Continued resistance training after summer may risk giving up endurance for fall head races. We don't know.

Assuming that winter and spring resistance training is beneficial, any resistance training will build muscle mass.   My wife, from her experience as a trainer, underlines the vast difference between individuals, in their body proportions, their flexibility, and their overall tolerance. Beware of any 'one size fits all' approach. Be sensitive to your body's feedback. Work with a qualified professional trainer for the most productive results.

It seems best to do exercises that replicate rowing movements, starting easy and remaining wary of twinges that signal danger. Heavy weights are counter-productive. An every-third-day routine gives time for 'hypertrophy', the adaptation of muscles to accept increased loads. After five or six days rest, you will have no gain: your muscles are back to where they were. Matt Brzycki's published work is recommended for intelligent advice on efficient muscle building and a wealth of references to research studies on strength training (search on "Matt Brzycki") – he manages the fitness center at Princeton, and remains a winning sprinter.

Resistance training carries a greater risk of injury than rowing. Good posture is important. Brzycki's advice steers clear of some dangers, like trying to determine your 'one rep max'. Refer to Dr Stuart McGill's "Ultimate Back Fitness and Performance" for knowledgeable advice on saving your back.

Sweat before starting resistance exercise. Warm up at least 10 minutes on an erg, an elliptical, or similar.

Stretching should follow, not precede, a gym workout. Crunching abs is good for stretching lower back muscles as well as strengthening your core.

One of my stretching exercises is mentioned here, only because someone else with hamstring issues might benefit. This is a two-handed heel lift, seated on the floor, placing both hands over the ball of one foot, and pulling the heel off the floor with the knee hyper-extended. It hurts in the first days, and some people can't do it at all. This stretch cured severe hamstring cramps.

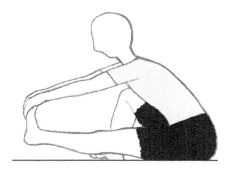

Most essays are intended to spread knowledge, but these words on strength contain more questions than answers. Could a great grant writer find money to fund a study about strength training for experienced rowers? Otherwise, the benefit remains "chicken soup".

Appendix II - Starting with the Mirror

1. Get a mirror, from a bike shop, from Chesapeake Rowing (on line), or from any other source.

   ... bike mirrors clip onto eyeglass stems. If the stems are thick, the clips won't fit. Thin stems may need tape to stabilize the mirror.

   Bike mirrors are small and close to the eye. Field of vision is OK, but the view is easily obscured by water drops from rain or backsplash, especially if water is also on eye glasses.

   ... Chesapeake Rowing's mirror stems fit into ¼" wire clips on a headband. The mirror is larger than bike mirrors, further from the eye, and preferred by myself. The position of the clips on the headband puts the mirror rather high – if this is annoying, the clips can be remounted to angle the mirror stem down about 10°, so that the center of the mirror is at eye level.

   ... bike mirrors or Chesapeake Rowing mirrors can be attached to a hat with a brim. ¼" wire clips are available in most hardware stores. The clips can be attached with small bolts. The hat can't be floppy, and some backing may be needed to stabilize the clips.

   If you have a big head (dimensionally) be sure the hat sits deep enough to keep wind from blowing it off. The Adams EF 101 cap is a suggestion. It has a long bill to shelter the mirror and glasses from wet, and a lanyard that you can attach to your shirt. (Search on Adams EF 101)

   ... mounting large bike or car mirrors on the boat adds unnecessary weight, and adds significantly to the frontal area presented to the wind. A mirror on each side can improve the blind areas to the sides, but, for head racing, the main concern is close to the course dead ahead.

2. Most rowers who race at the Head Of The Charles put the mirror on the port side (their right side facing aft), because of the Weeks bridge and Eliot turn buoys on the port side. Also, most right handed people have more flexibility to turn their head left, the direction they would look in the batter's box playing baseball, so their view to the right needs more help. The choice is really open.

3. Put on the mirror (mounted on glasses, head band, or hat) and adjust the angle so that you can see **your ear**. Only one eye will have this view, and you can shut the other eye. (Rowing with one eye shut is a bad idea, but I find myself doing it sometimes.)

4. In the boat, assume a normal rowing position on the recovery. **Turn your head** so that you can see **the bow** of the boat.

If your head is lined up fore and aft, you will not be able to see the

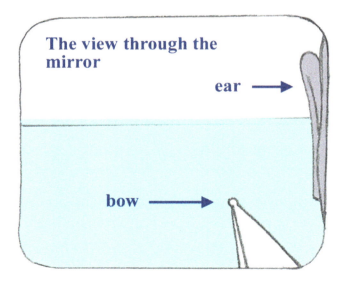

bow of the boat. You must turn your head, about 10°.

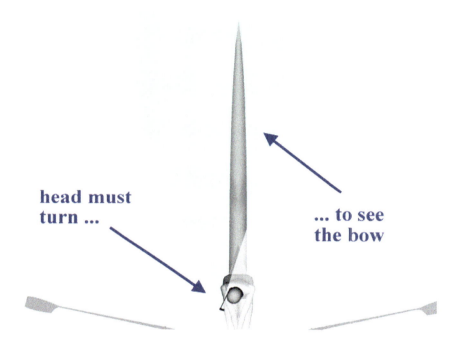

head must turn ... ... **to see the bow**

When you are steering the boat with the mirror you must see the bow. Otherwise, it's like driving a car looking out the side window. (Or, like landing a Corsair on an aircraft carrier, but that's another story).

5. Start rowing by swiveling your head and looking directly where you are going, before you refer to the mirror. While rowing (even after using the mirror becomes a habit) keep turning your head to check from side to side where the mirror is blind.

Line up the bow on a point ahead, and row toward it, with small changes in course to see what happens when you pull one oar more than the other. The goal is to make your will connect directly with the oars, so that you don't need to think.

6. Be prepared for pure misery in the first row, and several rows after. Don't get discouraged and quit. You are learning to break your right-means-right connection, and replace it with a right-means-left connection. Everyone suffers at first.

7. Most rowers go through a phase of disconnect, where they pull on the wrong oar to turn. If you see that the bow is turning in the wrong direction, **STOP**. Regroup, and start again. If you don't stop and insist on being right when you are wrong, you risk turning into trouble.

8. Count on at least two or three weeks for connecting the mirror to your reflexes. When you can steer by the mirror without needing to think, you can enjoy rowing with a permanent view of the water ahead. It's pleasant. You will row a shorter distance on a head racing course, and you will row faster without turning your body. Nobody reverts.

Appendix III – Stake Turn Technique

A "stake turn" is any sharp turn around a buoy. Ideally, more than one buoy will be set out, to alleviate congestion.

Stake turns put a premium on an easy-turning fin. Using any turn technique, an oversize fin will consume both time and energy.

Stopping the boat at the buoy(s) and hacking away, backing one oar and pulling the other, is inefficient and slow. Faster alternatives are:

...   'reverse feather' turn – flipping the inside oar backwards and using the reversed blade as a rudder

...   'row around' turn –rowing the boat in a big arc around the buoy(s), with sharp short pulls on the outside oar

The start of the row-around turn is very difficult to gauge properly. It must be initiated well outboard and before coming abeam of the buoy(s) or the big arc will carry the boat too far past.

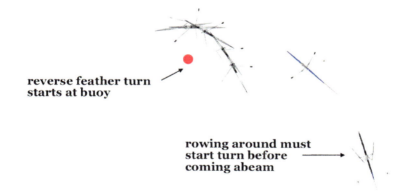

The reverse-feather turn is the surest and fastest way to turn the boat, but requires a learning process, described below. A well-executed reverse-feather turn can put you on the way home within 20 seconds from arrival at the turn mark.

Unfortunately, bow-mounted riggers or riggers with back stays prevent oars from trailing parallel to the boat. If you row a boat which does not permit the oars to trail, you must abstain from the reverse feather turn. Try rowing the boat around, it's faster than stop-and-hack.

Beginning racers should abstain from reverse feathering, if unsure of their balance.

The reverse feather technique uses momentum to turn the boat – 200+ lbs moving at 4 meters/second can apply far more turning pressure than arms hacking away at the water. The technique:

- ...   aim wide of the turn buoy until within 10 to 15 strokes distance.

- ...   angle in toward the buoy at about 30º. (Angling in is common to all stake turns.)

- ...   abreast of the buoy, **at the finish** of the last complete stroke, turn the inside oar backwards with a downward flip of the wrist. The flip only needs to engage the edge of the blade in the water; water pressure will snap the blade's face in the 'wrong' direction. Keep your layback, or the oar handle will be planted in your mid-section.

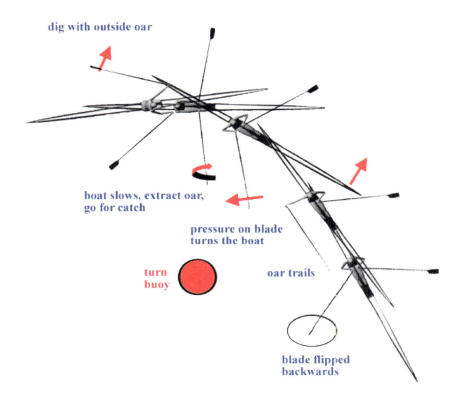

... if you are moving at full speed, you will not be able to keep the oar from trailing. Let it go parallel to the boat. Your hand will now be outboard at arm's length, with the oar handle cupped in the palm.

... pull in on the oar handle to push the stern sideways. Let the momentum of the boat do the work. Try to **keep the boat moving**. As long as the boat is moving, you will keep turning and making progress around the buoy.

... slowing to a near stop, the oar handle will be almost perpendicular to the boat. The boat's turn will be more than half way complete (30° approach + 60° reverse-feather turn). Keep your layback, to give room for swinging the handle inboard.

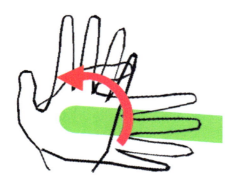

Extracting the reversed blade from the water is a natural movement.

As the hand pulls the oar handle back into the boat, the palm pivots around the oar handle. When the oar is more or less perpendicular to the boat, fingers can wrap around the handle.

When your fingers are able to grip the handle, give it a quick twist to spin the blade out of the water.

This is a strong, positive movement to free the blade.

... As soon as the inside oar is out of the water, slide forward to the catch. (Releasing the blade and sliding forward is a continuous movement.)

... Dig hard with the outside oar to get the boat moving again.

... after one or two hard, short strokes with the outside oar, the boat will have turned about 120º or 2/3 of the way around. With the forward momentum gained, repeat a reverse feather one more time. This will bring the boat around to 150º.

... release the inside blade and start rowing with both oars. Straighten out the remaining 30º of turn while gaining speed.

When you arrive at the turn buoy and start the turn, the blade must face backwards in order to cup the water and lock in – otherwise, at full speed, the rounded back of the blade will just skip out. Engagement of the reversed blade is not destabilizing. Instead, its firm bite in the water is like a brace. Even with the oar parallel to the boat, there is no impulse to capsize.

As long as the boat is moving, the flow of water over the curved back of the reversed blade will create lift, adding turn pressure to the force exerted by your arm.

Instinct resists reversing the blade while rowing at full speed. To learn:

...   stopped, with both oars feathered and blades flat on the water, swing one oar handle out, so the oar is parallel to the boat. You will be balancing on the other oar. It's not unnerving.

...   rowing slowly, flip one blade backwards and drop it in the water. Let the blade trail. You may feel some psychological resistance the first time you try. You will be surprised at how nicely the blade snaps into the water and how stable you feel with the blade locked in. It may help to start in shallow, warm water.

...   once the motion becomes familiar, increase speed until you are able to reverse the blade and bury it at full speed.

The reverse feather turn is so efficient, it can become a reflex for all turns. If it becomes a habit, watch out when you switch into a boat with backstays. The result can be ugly, with the oar wedged against the backstay so that it can't be moved. At full speed, you can bend a backstay.

A cautionary word about river current

At the Green Mountain Head in Vermont, and at Silverskiff in Italy, the stake turn is upstream. Current can be strong, especially after heavy rain.

Before starting to turn, it is safest to angle across toward the downstream side of the course. When you are past where the current will put you onto the turn buoy(s), execute the turn. The extra distance gives a margin of safety. Getting pinned against a buoy by a strong current is frustrating and time consuming.

Appendix IV – More About Fins

Slewing describes the tendency of a hull to turn more and more sharply once it departs from a straight line. The more the hull turns, the more the hull wants to turn (truly, a "vicious circle").

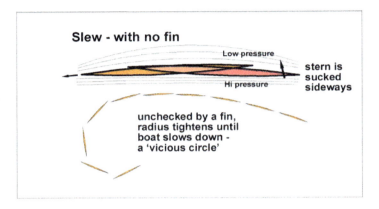

The fin should not let the boat slew at all. The boat's course should snap straight as soon as the oars are released from the water.

Wind drift is the effect of side winds pushing on the hull, oars, and rower. In addition to pushing the boat sideways, crosswinds effect steering. **Weather cocking** describes the bow or the stern being pushed away from the wind

In the following diagram, the blue hull at the bottom steers from A to B – easiest with a neutral fin (green), much more difficult if correction is needed for the bow being blown to leeward (red), more manageable if the bow turns toward the wind (orange).[4]

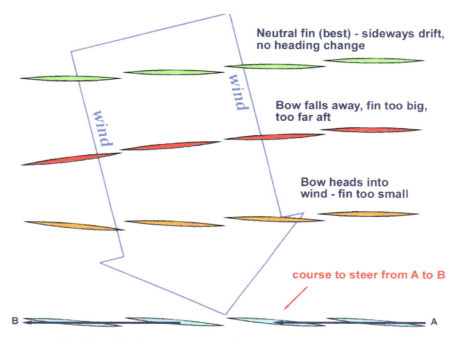

Heading offset to compensate for wind - easiest with neutral fin

Drift is the only concern for straight line racing. The yellow boat shows the most common steering effect of wind. That may be the reason for the over-large size of stock fins – to avoid weather cocking in cross winds.

The following diagram shows the lack of consensus among boat builders. Carl Douglas fins are the smallest, and his boats are the best in rough conditions. Large fins are more susceptible to being pushed around by waves and wakes. When the boat is moved by water that is disturbed beneath the surface, e.g. boat wakes and current eddies, **a large fin does not help**, and a small fin makes course correction easier.

Selected Stock Fins (1x)

4 cm

Carl Douglas 40° 66 cm²   Fluidesign 41° 93 cm²   Van Dusen 37° 99 cm²
Hudson 44° 85 cm²   Empacher 34° 98 cm²   Vespoli 62° 143 cm²

Submerged debris is a special concern in the fall head racing season, when storms rip tons of leaves off trees and storm drains carry all kinds of stuff into the water.

To be safe from picking up leaves, weeds, plastic bags, and other submerged hazards, a fin's leading edge should be **no more than 45° from horizontal**. At 60° or more, a fin is guaranteed to pick up stuff that it meets in the water. An amply angled fin will bounce over hard objects like sunken logs. A near-vertical fin is more vulnerable to damage, both to its leading edge and to the hull.

A fin survey cannot be complete without mention of Filippi's beautiful milled aluminum fin with a foil cross-section. It is small and deep, with sufficient rake angle to shed debris. Because it is milled and not cut from sheet, it is expensive. It is well worth its cost to replace the over-large Filippi standard fin that is shared by Filippi's 1x and 2x hulls.

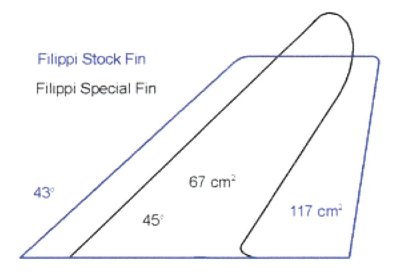

Rowers on the winding Charles River, especially rowers with cigar-shaped boats that are harder to turn, commonly cut away their stock fins. The following "Fin Fashion Gallery" shows a selection.

A Gallery of Fin Fashions - Cut for the Charles River

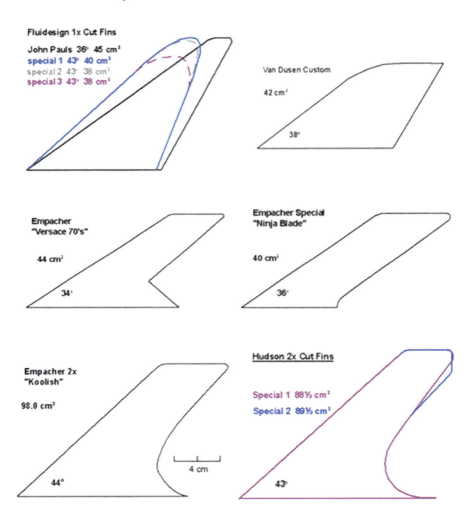

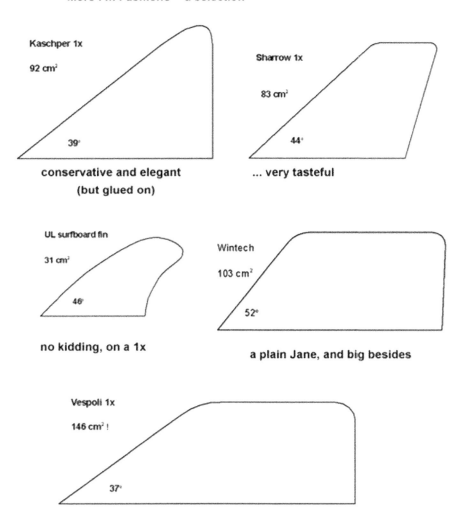

Appendix V – Course Notes

Armada Cup – Wohlensee, Switzerland (close to Bern)

Course length – 8,490 meters against a current.

Record holders – Men: Mahe Drysdale 32:24.3 (2009); Women: Emma Twigg 35:27.6 (2009)

Record speed – 4.08 m/sec = 0.5k pace 2:02.6; slow because of adverse current

Participants - ± 250

Strictly speaking, the Armada Cup is not a head race. 250 singles line up in 10 rows of 25 boats each, and start together with a cannon shot. At 700 meters the course rounds a sharp bend, where all boats converge. The bend sorts the fleet out. Boats emerge from the corner more or less lined up, as if they were in a head race.

Organizing Club – Rowing Club Bern (RCB) – at the finish line

Date – the last Saturday of October

Entries - Elites start in the front row, and many juniors (U23, U19, U17) are in back. It's a great opportunity for 16 year olds to measure their performance against Olympic medalists. Until recently, masters entries were relatively few, and 50+ was the oldest age division. Presently, a 60+ division has been added for men, although 50+ remains the upper age for women.

Search on "Armada Cup" for entry information.

Challenges

Getting around the first bend is hard. Racers in the front row can sprint for open water at the turn. For the rest, it's a problem with no good solutions. Dozens of boats close together churn up a rough chop. On the inside of the turn, hugging the bank can offer some safety, with a 90º turn needed to round the apex of the bend (stake turn technique works here). Otherwise it seems best to go way wide and avoid the chaos.

Past the first bend, the main hazard is weeds, an invasive species introduced (as the story goes) by a resident who dumped her tropical fish tank into the lake. The weeds float on and just below the lake's surface, forming a tangle that is impossible to row through.

An underwater lawnmower cuts a channel through the weeds. The Wohlensee is wide, and the mowed course is not always obvious. White buoys mark the channel in places, but at a distance the buoys are hard to distinguish from numerous white swans (who don't mind the weeds).

The last 2 kilometers wend their way up the mouth of the river Aare leading into the lake, with unnavigable shallows on the sides. These are marked and easier to avoid than the weeds.

Before the race, rowers embark at Rowing Club Bern and row down to the start area. The boating procedure is well organized, and rowers assigned to back rows are sent off a long time before the start. This means an extended wait in the start area, and needs ample provision for keeping warm and keeping hydrated.

Course Notes – North is to the left. Read from bottom up.

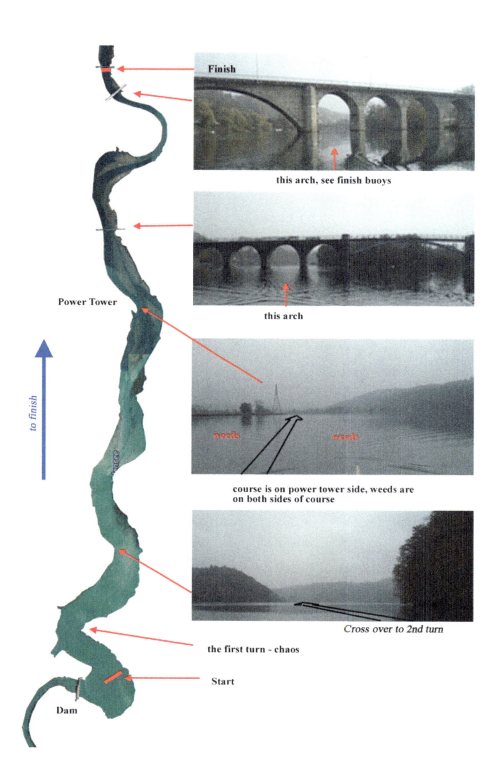

Appendix V (cont'd)

Silverskiff – Po River, Turin, Italy

Course Length –	10,390 meters (not 11km as claimed) with a stake turn upstream
Record holders –	Men: Mahe Drysdale 40:18.5 (2007); Women: Elisabetta Brugo 43:11.0 (2001)
Record speed -	4.27 m/sec = 0.5k pace 1:57.1
Participants -	500+ for Silverskiff, and another 170 U14's for Kinderskiff the day preceding

Date – the 1st or 2nd weekend of November. Saturday is for scullers 14 and under. Sunday is for racers aged 15+.

Organizing Club – Reale Società Canottieri Cerea (Cerea) – at the start/finish line.

Entries – Silverskiff now vies with the Scullers' Head of the River as the largest one-day regatta for single scullers. Including Kinderskiff, Silverskiff is the world's largest regatta for singles.

FISA divisions are observed through "I", and masters participation is strong. Silverskiff is unique among head races, in providing excellent singles (Filippi) at nominal cost. Boats available are limited: first come – first served with preference for distant visitors.

The start order is determined by the finish order in the preceding year. Racers without a time from the preceding year start behind, according to FISA divisions. Young rowers who have gained speed with the passage of a year can be expected to pass their elders, and first-year elites who start behind (Drysdale, Sinkovic, et al.) can be expected to pass dozens of rowers. If you want to race alongside an Olympic champion, this is the place to do it.

Search on "Silverskiff" for entry information. US rowers can contact John Flory at his Silverskiff email address: john.flory@silverskiff.org.

Challenges

The course is easy to navigate, and the main challenge is pacing for a very long row. Correct bridge arches are marked on panels approaching each bridge. In the heat of competition, the panels are not easy to see over your shoulder. Reconnaissance beforehand is recommended, as for all head races.

Current can be strong, and hugging the bank upstream is wise. On the way upstream, midway to the stake turn, course buoys dividing the river can leave little room for boats passing on the way upstream. Hugging the bank is clearly favored in this section (see course notes following*)*.

An adept stake turn is needed, being careful to avoid being swept down onto the turn buoys. It's a good idea to cross to the downstream side of the course before turning.

Course Notes:– North is at the top

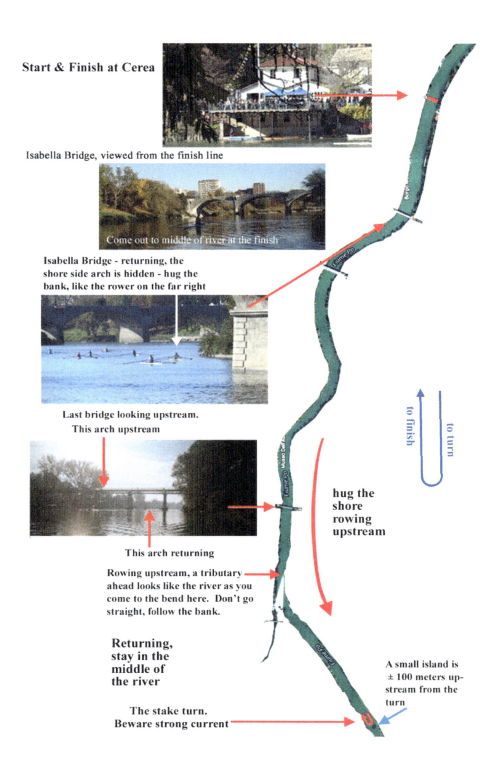

Approaching the last bridge before the finish, the arch closest to the shore (Cerea side) is hidden. Go through this arch, not the one that is visible, next out in the river. Approach the bridge about an oar's length off the bank (see photo above), and follow the bank around through the arch.

Current flows fastest at the center of the river. Coming downstream on the way home, stay away from the shore until the last bridge (Isabella Bridge), where the shore-side arch is quicker.

Parts of the course are not buoyed; coming downstream, be careful to stay outside of the upstream course on bends to starboard. From Isabella Bridge, come away from the bank into the middle of the river at the finish.

Prizes
In years past, Silverskiff awarded impressive 50 cm (20 in.) silver trophies in each division, but winners from distant lands had difficulty getting them home. More reasonably sized division trophies are now awarded. Male and female 1st, 2nd, and 3rd place finishers win gold coins, and many other prizes are offered.

Three-time winners are awarded this model of a 'silver skiff' with silver trimmings. A beautiful trophy, to celebrate a memorable experience on a very beautiful river.

This race is well worth a journey.

Appendix V – (cont'd)

The Head of the River – Tideway, London
Course length –   6,780 meters

The Head of the River is the grandfather of head racing events. The first regatta was held in 1926 with 20 eights competing. A women's race of just two boats followed in 1927.

Today, any crew, boat, gender or age can find a Head of the River race to contest, in one of eight separate events. Some row on shortened courses, and not all are always from Mortlake to Putney, West to East. The races are listed here:

Head of the River (men's eights, elite thru senior) – end of March
Veterans' Head (men, women, mixed eights) – day after elites
Women's Head of the River (elite thru Masters) – early March
Head of the River Fours (elite thru senior, 4-, 4+, 4x, men, women, mixed) – early November
Veterans' Fours Head (Masters 4-, 4+, 4x, men, women, mixed) – early November
Pairs Head (elite thru Masters, 2-, 2x, men, women, mixed) - early October
Schools' Head (school crews, 8+, 4+, 4-, 4x, boys, girls) – mid March
Scullers' Head - see below

Record holders –   Men's 1x: Mahe Drysdale   19:55.3(2006);
                          Women's 1x: G.Batten   21:41.1 (2002)
                          Men's 8+: British Nat'l Team 16:46.5 (1998)
                          Women's 8+: Composite   17:42.21(2014)

    Record speed - singles - 5.67 m/sec = 0.5k pace 1:28.2
                           eights - 6.74 m/sec = 0.5k pace 1:14.2

                           phenomenal speed owing to tidal flow

The notes below are devoted to the **Scullers' Head**; the channel is the same for all of the Head of the River events.

Participants - 500+ entries, less than 500 at the start
Date – the last Saturday of November, or the first Saturday of December, depending on the hour of the ebbing tide.

Organizing Club – Vesta Rowing Club – on the embankment at the Putney end, upstream from the finish line

Entries – This was the largest one-day regatta for single scullers, prior to the growth of Silverskiff. Possibly because of the daunting reputation of the Tideway, it remains a predominantly British regatta, with relatively few international entries. FISA divisions are observed through "I". Racers start in the order of the preceding year's finish, up to 140. Above that, the starting order is according to FISA divisions.

Search on "Vesta Rowing Club" for information.

Challenges

The ebbing tide is the challenge. The Tideway rises and falls over 15 feet. The water moves fastest immediately following the crest of the flood tide, and racing is timed to start at the moment the tide turns.

Boats are wet launched from embankments that slope down to the low water mark. Many rowers wear high rubber boots ("Wellies") which they stow in their boats. Launching barefoot, with subsequent donning of dry socks, is a possibility. Boats must be held against the tide while gathering oars. It helps to have a friend nearby.

Traffic rules are important to know and available on line and in print. Rules switch from flood tide to ebb tide, and change for race day. Read and heed. Materials refer to "Middlesex side" and "Surrey side' – the north and south sides of the river, or port and starboard when rowing downstream on the race course.

The race direction is downstream with the ebbing tide. The river is 160 meters across, and the channel is only 20 or 30 meters wide. Extensive flats, where the water moves slowly or not at all, lie on either side of the channel.

Staying in the current is not obvious, but necessary. Rowing onto the flats is like standing on the brakes. Course notes below are no substitute for trips on the river, either with a knowledgeable rower, or with a coach in a motorboat. Even with practice, it is easy for a visitor to get off course, out of the tide and into slack water.

Racers line up in start order, hugging the Surrey side, below Chiswick bridge. The line of boats progresses upstream against the tide through the Surrey side arch. The start area is well marshaled, and each racer is advised to turn-and-go, with a start interval of 5 or 6 seconds, through the center arch. Be alert. The goal is to launch as quickly as possible, to take advantage of the fastest moving tide. The entire fleet is headed downriver in little more than an hour.

Course notes: North is to the left, East is at the top. Read from bottom up.

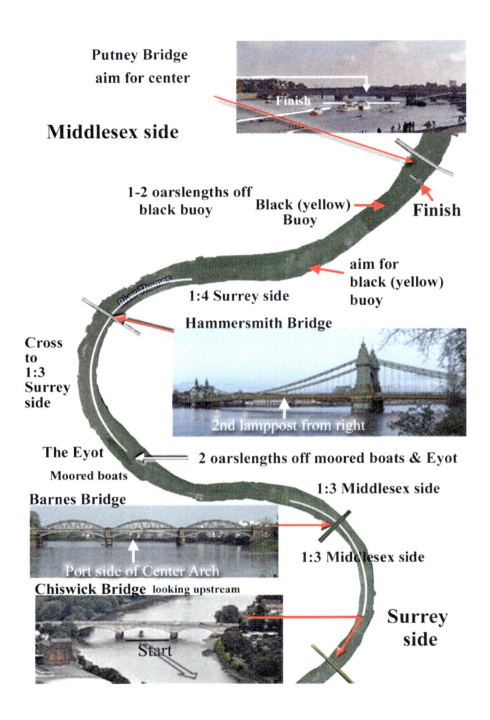

The first bend from Chiswick to Barnes Bridge tempts to turn in toward the Middlesex bank. Instead, maintain 1:3 distance off the Middlesex side to stay in the channel, and go through the port side of the center arch of Barnes Bridge (there is some disagreement among local experts, with conflicting advice to go through Barnes Bridge at the center.)

If north winds are blowing into the stretch between Barnes Bridge and the Eyot, waves stand up against the tide. Rowing through the standing waves is like being dragged upstairs. With wind from the southwest, water is smooth. With the added speed of the tide, the scenery goes by at an astonishing rate while passing the Eyot at two-oars' distance.

The most difficult section – for me – is between the Eyot and Hammersmith Bridge. The channel crosses to pass under the "2nd lamppost" on Hammersmith Bridge, about 1:3 on the Surrey side. With no point ahead to aim for, it is easy to be late crossing over.

The famous "black buoy", painted yellow, is sixty strokes from the finish. Pass close by the black (yellow) buoy and then come away from the line of boats, aiming at the center of Putney Bridge.

The finish is before the bridge. Continue to the bridge, turn to Surrey side and return inside the moored boats.

Low tide at the embankment upstream from the finish

Appendix V – (cont'd)

The Head Of The Charles® – Charles River, Cambridge

Course length –	4,650 meters - 4,800 meters for most rowers
Records –	Men's 1x: Andrew Campbell 17:11.6 (2014); Women 1x: Kathleen Bertko 18:33.0 (2013) Men's 8+: US Nat'l Team 13:58.9 (1997) Women's 8+: US Nat'l Team 15:26.6 (2007)
Record speed -	singles - 4.50 m/sec = 0.5k pace 1:51.0 eights - 5.60 m/sec = 0.5k pace 1:29.3
Participants -	10,000+ total, theoretically limited to 500 singles, but more singles raced in 2014
Date –	the third weekend in October.

Organizing Club – based at Cambridge Boat Club, the Head Of The Charles Regatta is a freestanding organization with a permanent year-round staff.

Entries – The Head Of The Charles is the world's largest rowing regatta. Its singles entries, spread over two days of racing, exceed the number at Scullers' Head of the River and Silverskiff. Masters are well represented in all age groups through FISA "J" (although FISA divisions apply only for 60+ events, and a melange of names is applied to all divisions). For scullers, doubles events are offered as well as singles. The regatta turns away roughly half of applicant entries. Places for first-time applicants, and for previous participants with times 5% more than the prior year's winner, are filled by a lottery. To be ensured of a place, a finish within 5% of the winner's time is needed in the preceding year.

Special "Directors'" sculling events are offered for quads (men's, women's, and mixed), mixed doubles, and parent-child doubles. Entry fees are elevated in support of the regatta's endowment. Entries are accepted on a first-come, first-served basis, and are limited to experienced crews (steering a quad on the course requires both course knowledge and skill.)

Paste www.HOCR.org in your web address line, for information.

Challenges

Completing the course in only 4,650 meters is an issue. Most visitors will cover 4,800 meters or more (i.e. losing more than half a minute). Accurate steering requires constant attention.

Diagrams in the preceding Navigation and Traffic sections are drawn from the Head Of The Charles course. They illustrate a few challenges that may be encountered, but far from all.

The full length of the course is monitored by teams of umpires stationed at key locations. Many parts of the course are buoyed, and cutting a buoy earns a penalty: 5 seconds for the 1st, and 10 seconds for subsequent. Avoiding buoys is a challenge in itself.

Boats tend to cluster on the best line, because the course is narrow and defined by bridge arches and banks. Avoiding other boats, while passing or being passed, is more of an issue here than in other head races. Right-of-way infractions are noted by the umpires, who may impose time penalties or disqualifications for serious collisions. The umpires do not wish to penalize or eject boats, and light interplay is usually tolerated.

The regatta's rules for passing are sensible, and are included at the end of this section.

Late October weather is highly variable in New England, and winter-like conditions can present an additional challenge. Only one regatta was cancelled, for dangerous current following storm rains; another was shortened by 1/3, to start upstream in sheltered water above the basin. In recent years, pleasant weather has prevailed.

Course notes: North is right, West is up– read from bottom to top

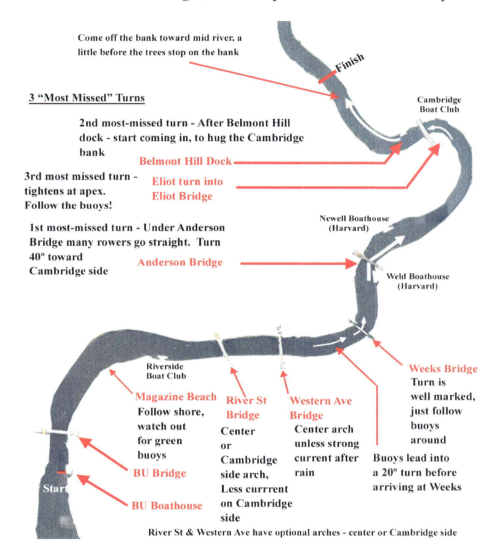

Normally, current on the race course is negligible, and neither side is favored. After heavy rain, the Cambridge side is favored on the straight from Riverside Boat Club to past Western Avenue. The rhumb line from Riverside Boat Club to Weeks Bridge would go directly through the piling dividing the arches of River Street Bridge - a choice is necessary. Most rowers take the center arch of both bridges, some take the Cambridge arch of River Street Bridge, and the center arch of Western Avenue Bridge, which may be the best route.

The tight turn at Weeks Bridge is easy to follow, but beware of boats converging from the Cambridge side, who have missed the 20º turn leading into Weeks Bridge.

The first and second "most missed" turns, at Anderson Bridge and at Belmont Hill dock, are missed by so many rowers because the course straight ahead looks OK. It's not. Lapsed attention here costs many seconds.

The third "most missed" turn, into Eliot Bridge, tightens drastically at the apex and requires a vigorous effort to stay with the diminishing arc of the buoys. Unlike the first two, this missed turn has disastrous consequences, leading into the Cambridge side pilings of Eliot Bridge. Especially at this turn, beware of rowers ahead who have gone wide, converging in an effort to pass through the center arch.

The course around the Eliot bend continues turning to port until under Eliot Bridge, where you pick up a line to the green course marker off the Belmont Hill dock.

The Head Of The Charles website includes an excellent narrative for steering the course, by Geoffrey S. Knauth, a Cambridge Boat Club rower and former US National Team coxswain. Paste on your web address line:

http://www.hocr.org/the-regatta/competitors/rules-and-regulations/steering-the-head-of-the-charles/

The picture below is a joke, showing the Charles River course if all the turns were to starboard – A more measured calculation shows 413° of major turns, excluding small course adjustments.

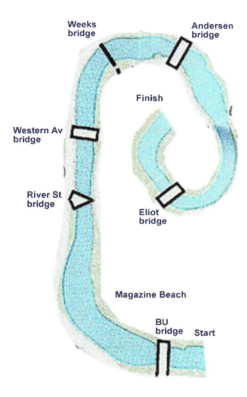

The Head Of The Charles "Competitors" pages on line, concerning "Rules and Regulations", provide detailed race guidelines along with the various penalties for infractions.

Section 12, including common-sense advice about passing, is relevant to this book's sections on Navigation and Tactics. Section 12 is copied below, with permission.

Head Of The Charles Rules and Regulations (excerpt)   Section C – Guidelines and Responsibilities.

12:   General Responsibilities (guidance to crews and scullers)

The Charles River is a narrow course with many tight turns. Good sportsmanship is expected at all times and costly penalties have been assigned in the past in cases of bad sportsmanship. The ability to accomplish effective and safe passing is an important aspect of successful racing. However there are many situations when passing cannot be accomplished safely due to traffic congestion and physical obstacles. The following are the basic responsibilities of scullers and crews in these situations:

12.1. Responsibility of Overtaking Boat (Passer): The boat overtaking (Passer) has the right of way to pass (on the side of its choice) if a safe pass can be accomplished. However, crews and scullers must take note of the following:

(A)   If a pass is attempted and there is not adequate room and time to perform the pass, the Passer is at risk of incurring interference penalties.

(B)   In situations involving three and more boats, there are areas such as bridge arches and narrow, tight turns where passing cannot be accomplished safely. In these situations, the Passer must be prudent and delay the act of passing until the pass can be accomplished without incident. The wise sculler or crew knows that more time can be lost by pressing a situation rather than by slowing down and waiting for the right moment to pass.

(C)   Communicate effectively during racing. All shells with bow-loaded coxswains are strongly advise to have their bow seat notify the coxswain when there is clear water astern after completing the pass. Timely instruction from the bow seat rower may assist the Passer's coxswain in avoiding stern-to-bow collision and/or an interference penalty due to cutting in too soon.

(D) When boats come together and interlock, this does not necessarily result in a penalty situation if there were no specific violations of the racing rules (section 10).

12.2. Responsibility of Overtaken Boat (Overtakee):

The boat being overtaken (Overtakee) must yield and give suitable room to the Passer (on the side chosen by the Passer) if a safe pass can be accomplished. Generally this will be the shortest line that gives an advantage. Failure to yield to the Passer is one of the most serious infractions of competitive conduct. Crews and scullers must:

(A) Be alert to possible upcoming passing attempts and promptly yield when there is adequate room and time.

(B) Be prepared to miss a few strokes to allow the Passer to pass safely and without interference.

(C) Communicate effectively during racing. All shells with bow-loaded coxswains are strongly advised to have their bow seat rower notify the coxswain if a following crew is about to make a pass and on which side the passer is approaching. Timely instruction from the bow seat rower may assist the coxswain in avoiding an interference penalty.

12.3. Safety:

Respect for the safety of other competitors and their equipment must be observed at all times. At no time should an oar be used in anger toward another crew or competitor.

This regatta offers so much, as a celebration of the sport, that just rowing the course is good for the soul. Participation isn't only about medals. Still, this is one to be happy about.

CPSIA information can be obtained at www.ICGtesting.com
Printed in the USA
BVOW07s1426051015

420835BV00003B/3/P